Seeking
And
Enjoying
The
True Treasure
Of
This Life

Paula Matthews

Spirit & Life
Publications SM

Seeking And Enjoying The True Treasure
Of This Life

©2013 Paula Matthews
Cover by: Paula Matthews

Illustrator: Danielle N. Scott

All rights reserved. No part of this book may be reproduced in any
Form by any electronic or mechanical means including
Photocopying, recording, or information storage and retrieval
Without permission in writing from the author.

Unless otherwise noted, all scripture in this book was taken From The
Holy Bible King James Version
(Public Domain)

Scripture taken from The Message.
Copyright © 1993, 1994, 1995, 1996, 2000, 2001, 2002.
Used by permission of NavPress Publishing Group.

Published by
Spirit & Life Publications[SM]
Shaker Heights

ISBN: 978-0-9851172-9-0

Printed in the United States

*To my nieces, Danielle Scott and six-year old Jordyn Hawk,
Priceless Gems In The Making.*

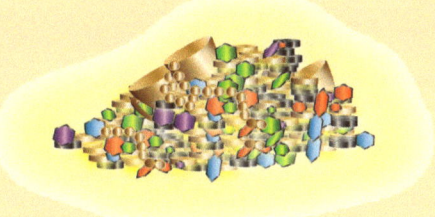

**It Is The Glory Of God
To Conceal A Thing:
But The Honour Of Kings
Is To Search Out A Matter.**

Proverbs 25:2 (KJV)

CONTENTS

AUTHOR'S NOTE   15
On Seeking Great Treasure   15

PREFACE   19
The Paradigm Shift   19
Meet The Holy Spirit; Your Guide   23

INTRODUCTION   27
What Is True Treasure?   27
My Adventure To Eden   33

THE TREASURE HUNT BEGINS NOW! 35

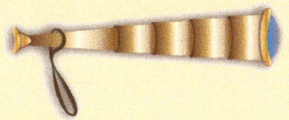

CONCLUSION   81
Protecting Your Treasure From Pirates   81

**Eye Hath Not Seen, Nor Ear Heard,
Neither Have Entered
Into The Heart Of Man,
The Things Which God Hath Prepared
For Them That Love Him.**

I Corinthians 2:9 (KJV)

Author's note
On Seeking Great Treasure

King Solomon said that God has made everything beautiful in its own time; that God placed the world in the hearts of men and yet men could never figure it out (Ecclesiastes 3:11). Solomon was considered the wisest man who ever lived, but the answer to this mystery of the world was not made known to him. The Creator God has indeed placed within every human heart the desire for the eternal (immortality); a desire to forge an unforgettable path of existence that would leave its mark for generations to come. Most of us have fumbled through this life in search of that elusive path of destiny, but few will ever find it because it is shrouded in a mystery hidden by God before the foundation of the world. Psychics and soothsayers will never find it. Astrologers will never find, nor will horoscopes predict the things that belong only to God. It so pleased God, that he has hidden these things from the wise and prudent of this world. These are the secret things that belong to God. He reveals them to his people as part of their inheritance (Deuteronomy 29:29).

On February 25, 2013, the Lord began unfolding the mystery of what he called **"the kingdom within us"** and **"the treasure in earthen vessels."** He said, **"Eye has not seen it. It is revealed by the Spirit."** King Solomon saw the mystery but he was not aware that God desired to share this mystery by his Spirit. The Lord said that he has **"Set eternity in the hearts of men, that is only revealed by the Spirit and activated by our faith."** The world that God has placed within the hearts of men is the Kingdom of God. It is a world that operates in a manner that is vastly different than what we know in the world today. The Kingdom of God is a supernatural kingdom. One that operates by laws that are strictly governed by God. Even the purpose of life in the Kingdom is vastly different from our typical view of the world. Take Christianity for example. Most people think of it as a religion, but in God's Kingdom it is a way of living. In fact, Christianity is called a *"new and living way* (Hebrews 10:20)." Throughout the book of Acts, Christianity is referred to as *"the way," "the way of God"* or *"the way of the Lord."*

When Jesus walked the earth he preached about the kingdom. He even told people that he was *"the way* (John 14:6).*"* Again, most people would tell you that Jesus was talking about religion and becoming a Christian, but Jesus hated religion. He fought against the religious rulers of his day because of their false doctrines, traditions and hypocrisy. They were stuck on religion and the Law of Moses. When Jesus came preaching about a way of living and a way of loving each other and loving God, the church leaders accused him of *"perverting the nation"* with his teachings (Luke 23:2). How could teaching about loving God and loving your neighbor pervert a nation? This is how religion twisted Christianity in ancient times, as it still does to this day. So if not religion, what did God design for Christianity and for humans in general?

God is love. Everything he ordains and purposes for mankind is based upon his love for us. God never invent religion, humans did. God created men to be kings and priests who would reign in this life. God created men not so that they could go to heaven, but that they would experience days of heaven on the earth. The Lord had me go back to my prayer journal dated 2009-2010. In that journal I found an amazing prophecy. The Lord told me it was time to release it to his people. The prophecy was about **"The Restoration of An Ancient Kingdom Dynasty"** in the earth. God said that he was about to, **"Raise a nation in the earth; a nation of those who are obedient to God. Power and glory shall be unto all who obey for it is the Glory of God Manifest in Men."**

Here is the amazing thing about this prophecy. The Lord said that those who would find the treasure within, would become partakers of this great dynasty of wealth and power in the earth. In fact, their particular treasure would display their share of God's great dynasty in the earth. According to God, this ancient dynasty that is being restored in the earth would resemble the wealth and power that God gave to Adam at creation. We are talking about unlimited supernatural power and immense wealth without the corruption we see in the world today. Unlike the world economy we see today, in God's kingdom dynasty, power and wealth never diminish. This wealth and power has the supernatural ability of God to multiply at whatever rate is necessary to rid the earth of all poverty and oppression. So where has it been? It has been hidden in this earth for over two thousand years, waiting to be discovered by men.

Remember that Jesus said he was the way to the kingdom. He told us to live as he lived. He demonstrated the kingdom in all he said and did. Whatever human issue he encountered, Jesus applied the kingdom solution. Jesus dealt with health issues, taxes, poverty and starvation, marital issues, prostitution, elder abuse, spouse abuse, adultery, pornography (lust and fornication), mental health, spiritual and physical death. Jesus also demonstrated the kingdom power over the weather and over nature. He gave this same power to the church and told them to occupy until he returns. So, what happened? They did not want this man to rule over them and they went their own way (Luke 19:14). Men began chasing after religion and not after God. God only reveals his secrets to those who diligently seek him. So while the world has been suffering from poverty, disease and degradation, those calling themselves Christians have been idly watching the earth diminish under the curse not understanding that their obedience to what Jesus commanded would bring every solution this earth needs.

"God's kingdom has always been about changing the lives of human beings by ridding the earth of hunger, sickness, disease, poverty and human degradation. This is Christianity! It's not a Religion. It's a way of living; a way of loving and sharing with our fellow man." This is the message that has been revealed by the Spirit. The Lord wants to manifest the kingdom in the lives of men in righteousness, peace and joy unspeakable and full of glory.

The Lord said that becoming part of this dynasty is available to anyone who would obey his instructions, with one stipulation. It must ***"Be sought after as one who searches for great treasure."*** So, how does one search for great treasure? Treasure hunters search with a passion for adventure, with their eyes open to any possible trap or peril along the way. This is quite similar to what you will learn in this book. We have provided step-by-step instructions with intent of instilling passion for seeking God's kingdom treasures. We will also inform you of the possible setbacks, traps and scoundrels during your search. We even share information to help you deal with pirates lying in wait to steal your treasure once it has been obtained. There is also a treasure map with icons along each step of the hunt. Each icon symbolizes a single step along our path to find your treasure that corresponds to a chapter that gives even more details.

Please understand that each person has a unique treasure awaiting them. While we do provide a map and instructions. They only serve as an example of your actual course to your specific treasure. We want to show you how to navigate through to the treasure, but depending on what kind of treasure awaits you, there may be additional steps and precautions needed on your part. Use this book as a template for your own treasure hunt. Let the Holy Spirit guide you to create your very own treasure hunt. The Holy Spirit knows the specifics of what God has for your life. He also knows all the traps and entanglements that you will encounter on your journey. The Holy Spirit is a priceless treasure in himself because he also knows how to circumvent any encumbrance along the way. Rely on his expertise, not your own, and you will find your way to success.

With all this said, enjoy your adventure . . . and, just so that you know, there will be many more such adventures and more treasure to seek, if you so choose! We pray that reading this book will increase your hunger and thirst for uncovering the mysterious secrets of the kingdom!

PREFACE
The Paradigm Shift

Taking on a treasure hunt of the kingdom magnitude is more than just a notion. You can expect great treasure and much adventure; which includes both perils and villains. The difference between this and other treasure hunts is that you are traversing time and space in the kingdom endeavor. Therefore, the treasure you obtain carries a priceless value in heaven and in the earth, and it increases in value over the generations. Whatever you obtain becomes your good treasure and an inheritance for your children's children to a thousand generations.

You can expect to be operating in both the spiritual and the physical realms of reality. Many times it will be done simultaneously and without your full knowledge of what's going on around you. This is not unusual. We are dealing with spiritual laws, many of which are encased in many more mysteries. That is why it is necessary to have a spiritual guide. The Holy Spirit knows the laws and he will guide you along the correct route even if he doesn't explain the process. No matter what he says; obey his instructions and the supernatural realm will automatically take over. Now, I did mention perils and villains. They will also becoming from both realms. Most times the Holy Spirit will seem to ignore what's going on in the physical realm. Do not be alarmed. He knows that taking care of issues on the spiritual realm first, always eliminates what is going on in the physical or natural realm.

If you look at the most miraculous stories in the Bible, ordinary men always faced an impossible foe and they won. In the physical realm this is almost impossible, but with God's kingdom in operation, nothing is impossible. So don't be spooked by evil forces that come against you. They are reduced to only shadows when the Holy Spirit is your guide (Psalm 23). How else could young David find the courage to take on Goliath? Or how did Joshua lead the people to walk around the walls of Jericho and the walls fall down? Even Peter walked on water after Jesus told him to "come." The key to the miraculous is to turn your fear into faith. Faith can only come when you hear a word of instruction from the

Lord. If he is commanding you, just obey what he says and you'll soon be turning water to wine. Don't be surprised that these are impossible feats in the physical realm. The Kingdom of God operates in the realm that seems impossible for men. When you find your treasure it will also seem to be of impossible proportions. It's supernatural. Don't worry about what you don't understand. This is not an intellectual competition. This is faith; the God kind of faith. This is how all the heroes of the Bible operated. For generations people have only thought these to be amusing and fascinating stories. When you begin operating in the spiritual realm with the Holy Spirit, you will soon become aware of the unlimited power and wisdom available to ordinary men who dare to go after the kingdom.

There is also a special purpose attached to this treasure that you should know about. We are in a very unique season in history. God has something to prove to the world. That is one of the reasons he is offering this hunt for his kingdom treasure. We mentioned the kingdom dynasty, but since this dynasty has been lying dormant in the earth, things have to be resurrected from within every physical and spiritual dimension of the earth. This could mean turbulence and upheaval on every realm.

The Lord showed me a vision in which the earth and the heavens surrounding the earth were violently convulsing. There was a spiritual transformation that was manifesting in the geological fabric of the earth. It was as though the earth was regurgitating all the garbage and evil of this earth. At the same time great treasure was being unearthed around the globe. Things that God had hidden even since the Garden of Eden, were now resurfacing on the earth. Precious minerals and gems and fresh untouched resources were coming from deep inside the earth's core. The earth looked like a giant Rubik's cube as sections turned inside out revealing entirely new and more beautiful surfaces. It was like beauty from beneath the ashes and ruin caused by the earth's spewing. This transformation touched every aspect of human life on every continent. The Lord said that he is demanding earth to give up her secrets both the bad and the good. He is going to prove that the secret things belong to him. This is a blessing for the honest treasure seeker, but it can prove harmful to those who operate in corruption. Whatever we hidden God will expose. It will be exposed during this season.

Here is the word the Lord gave me, *"I am who I've said I am. I am God and I change not! But have you listened to my servants the prophets who have declared to you what I am doing in this season? I will destroy your human wisdom. Have I not created this earth for my purpose? Why then do you continue to ignore what I have created to prosper you? Why have you sought your own way? I will bring your way to an end says God. For I will prove once and for all that I am that great I AM and besides me there is none other who loves and purposes for you a great harvest of goodness and mercy and compassion and wealth that would last an eternity. But you would not listen nor take heed to my voice."*

"America, I will prove my power and my love on behalf of those who still believe and were faithful to me. Watch and learn of me as I move upon them and prosper them with all my good. Don't be jealous for what I have given to them is reward for their faithfulness to my purpose. That purpose still remains for you. If you would listen and obey my voice. This is my purpose and it shall be done in this earth. I am God have I not said it, shall I not also bring it to pass?"

As you can see, God definitely has something to prove, which is why he commanded me to write this book. There is something coming upon the earth and it will take a paradigm shift just to manage. You beloved are being called to a much higher level of performance in this hour. The Kingdom of God is more than about money and wealth, it is about prospering all human life on earth. To accomplish this purpose in the earth, it is going to take both supernatural power and money. Money is a sore subject in the church, and many think it a sin to have wealth and riches. God keeps bringing to my attention his purpose for the wealth. While writing this book, the Lord told me to do research on the wealthiest people in the world. I searched the latest listing of billionaires. He had me study every person closely. Then a few days the later the Lord gave me the following vision that left me breathless. *In a vision the Lord showed me a billionaires list. He let me see every face from the top to the bottom of the list. Then the Hand of the Lord swiped the list clean from top to bottom and the Lord filled up a new list that was much longer than previous lists. There were not only more billionaires than ever, but individually they seemed to have more billions than those from the past. It was though immeasurable amounts of wealth just came out of thin air. The Lord said that he is about to unveil the treasures of dark-*

ness and the riches hidden in secret places. Some had been hidden by evil men. Other treasures had been reserved by God since the foundation of the earth and slated for release to prosper his people in our life time; and the wealth of the wicked will be given to the just. **"The secret things belong to me," says God. "I will expose that which is hidden in the earth; every unknown resource and bounty. I will also expose every lying scheme and plot against men in the earth; the lies and plots against my people." "What was done in the dark will be brought into the light. That which was spoken in closets in secret will be shouted on the rooftops. Likewise every secret plan I will reveal to my people to make clear their inheritance." "I will manifest my secret wish to bless and proposer you this day! Yes, the secret things belong to me," says God. "And I will reveal them all: both bad and good."**

God sacrificed everything to provide this treasure for men. Jesus gave his life so that we could have access to this treasure. You will also learn, that if you want to obtain this treasure it will cost you everything as well. Is it worth it? Decide for your self, but in my experience there is nothing that can be compared to obtaining the infinite power, riches, wisdom, strength, honor, glory and blessings of God's kingdom. Walking in the mysteries of God catapults you into the realm of what humans would call the impossible; but it is anything but impossible. This is the realm where **all things are possible.** In this mysterious realm we are able to do all things THROUGH CHRIST; in the power of God's might because we operate in the unsearchable and immeasurable wisdom and power of God's kingdom. It didn't take me long to abandon all that I had known in the past and go for this treasure. It has been the most exhilarating adventure of my life. I wouldn't trade it for anything or anyone. For the first time in my life I found something that had only one qualification; **I had to believe and walk out that belief by faith.** It was presented to me as an open invitation to a life without limits, and the same is available to each of you today. If you still have a thirst for adventure, come follow me as we introduce your guide for this journey.

Meet The Holy Spirit; Your Guide

Some people cringe when you mention the Holy Spirit; and if you say the Holy Ghost others may run in fear. Unfortunately, in the church there are many misconceptions about the Holy Spirit. First of all, the Holy Ghost is just another name for the Holy Spirit. He is neither a ghost nor a spirit in the way most humans think. The Holy Spirit is person. He is considered the breath of God. He is also referred to as the wind or mind of God. People tend to get the person of the Holy Spirit confused with his manifestations. I grew up in a Baptist church where the people had a fear of the Holy Ghost and they shunned anyone who spoke in tongues. Even though the Bible taught that tongues were one of the evidences of operating in the Holy Spirit. I distinctly remember being told as a child that tongues were from the devil. There was one woman in our Baptist church who spoke in tongues and I would stare at her trying to figure it all out. She was a sweet, kind and loving woman who spoke loving things about God and Jesus while coming in and out of tongues. How could this be the devil? It just didn't make sense to me. There were also times that I would hear a song in church and something would move deep inside of my heart, and when this woman would speak in tongues it was as though something alive was fluttering in my heart as well.

While I never spoke in tongues in the Baptist church, the Holy Spirit did move mightily in my life and it wasn't long before I too was labeled as the devil. At the time I didn't understand it, but I began prophesying at a very young age. My family called me a baby fortune teller, until someone told them fortune tellers were from the devil. Rather than praying to God, or reading what the Bible said about my gift, my parents called me the devil. The saving grace in my life came from my great grandmother who intimately knew the Holy Spirit. She could hear the voice of God clearly and when she spoke about him, it always touched my heart in a powerful way. It was this powerful matriarch of the family that recognized my gifts and encouraged me to allow the Holy Spirit to lead my life. My heart was yearning for more and years later, the Lord would send me to Los Angeles where I was surrounded by charismatic

Christians from many different denominations. I always thought that these Pentecostal types would be far advanced spiritually because they believed in the Holy Spirit. Then, I saw something that concerned me deeply. Many of them had begun to reduce the Holy Spirit to a feeling that made them run around the church and screaming and speaking in tongues. These people would run, scream, spit, spin around and leave the church with demons, sickness, poverty and disease. On the surface, they pretended to be holy, sanctified and saved, but so many of them were dealing with the same devils that plagued the outside world. They were very religious in their dress and mannerism but their hearts were full of evil. They had rejected the holiness of the Holy Spirit and substituted a strict form of religion (Later in this book I will share the lesson the Lord taught me about how secrets things in the human heart will hinder the work of the Holy Spirit and defile the individual).

Here is the thing about the Holy Spirit. Since he is God, you must be careful how you treat him and how you address him. Be careful never to criticize spiritual manifestations that you don't understand, or you run the risk of blaspheming God. Even while I observed crazy behavior in the Pentecostal churches, I never criticized the people openly. I took all my questions directly to God so I could learn more about how he operated. Unfortunately, many Christians are quick to call people the devil. So many people in the church don't know God nor do they recognize the Holy Spirit. They call that which is holy, profane and they defile the holiness of God. It's like calling bad, good and what's good, bad. The Holy Spirit is God. He is also called the Spirit of Truth because he communicates only truth to our hearts; but God's people often reject the truth because it is not convenient. A lie suits the motives of their evil hearts. The truth on the other hand, may hurt you in order to heal you. It's God's tough love.

Not every word the Holy Spirit speaks will be pleasant, but it will be beneficial, especially if you want to obtain your treasure. Also know that whatever the Holy Spirit speaks will always be consistent with the nature and character of God. It may not come directly from the pages of the Bible (although much of it will), but the Holy Spirit will never say, or instruct you to do anything that is contrary to God's will for your life. It may be something very different from what other people are doing. That's okay. Your course is specific to what God has for you; and just because the Holy Spirit tells you to do something doesn't make it right for someone else. The path is narrow and there are specifics designed for each of us. This is why a close relationship with the Holy Spirit is necessary. He knows the specific plan for each of us.

Reverence the Holy Spirit and make him your best friend. Again, he is God. He is the third person of the Godhead. The Lord explained the Godhead to me in this manner. God the Father is a spirit (John 4:24). God the Son (Jesus) was his body (John 1:14) and God the Holy Spirit is his mind. Together the Father, Son and Holy Spirit are one being. They can never be separated and they will always agree with one another. They are one. God also created man in his likeness and image. We are speaking spirits that reside in a physical body, and we also have a mind (soul). We should be one in all of our parts just like the father, son and Holy Spirit. Jesus' greatest prayer was that we all would be one in spirit just like he and the Father and the spirit were one (John 17:20-23). This can only happen when one is determined to follow the instructions of the Holy Spirit. Our obedience aligns us perfectly with the will of God for our lives. We will also talk more about aligning ourselves with God's will. It involves regeneration and being conformed into the original image created for man. For now, we just want to focus on the identity of the Holy Spirit. We will talk in depth about his important role in your obtaining the treasures of the kingdom.

Please notice that unless I am quoting scripture verbatim, I will routinely use the name Holy Spirit or Spirit of God because it is consistent with how the name was used in the Old Testament. The name Holy Ghost does not appear until the New Testament and even then, the two names are used interchangeably. In fact, the Holy Spirit is the same Spirit of God that moved upon the face of the deep at creation. The Holy Spirit is the Spirit of Truth (John 16:13), the Comforter (John 14:16) and Guide (John 16:13). He is also called the Mind of Christ (I Corinthians 2:16) which is why the Holy Spirit is the perfect person to guide your journey to unlocking the mysteries of God. He searches the deep things of God and is responsible for revealing those things to you.

One last thing you should know. If you want the Holy Spirit to guide, you must employ him. He won't step into your life unless you invite him in. He will also only guide, if you operate by the laws of faith. We will also talk more about this later. The key to your success is this:

whatever the Holy Spirit says, do it! Don't try to figure it out. This is the supernatural plan of God. God's plans are bigger than you could ever imagine. Do not lean to your own understanding. In all your ways acknowledge him and he will direct your path (Proverbs 3:5-6). Do as he says. Move as the spirit moves. He is like the wind that blows. You'll hear his sound and not be able to tell where he has come from nor where he is going (John 3:8). This is how it is for those who follow the spirit. It is an adventure like none other known to man. So, sit back and let the Holy Spirit steer you on to success!

INTRODUCTION
What Is True Treasure?

When one thinks of treasure the first things that come to mind are wealth, jewels, precious metals and gems, or collector's items. The image of a pirate's treasure would capture the imagination of adventurous minds. While shady schemers might envision cold hard cash stashed away in mattresses or in secret bank accounts in far away lands. For sentimental hearts treasure may mean memories gathered in photographs, or souvenirs of times gone by; safely tucked away in scrapbooks and old storage chests. We all have treasures that we value and hold close to our hearts. However, there are very special treasures awaiting those with a pure heart to discover truth and uncover riches hidden in secret places. God has a storehouse full of mysteries and treasures that he desires to reveal to his people. For those who delight themselves in his word, he promises to give them treasures in the form of desires that he places within their hearts.[1] The secret things belong to God, but that which he reveals belong to his children as an inheritance. [2] These are the mysteries of God given to us to unveil and demonstrate in this earth. This is the Kingdom of God within us: the plan and purpose of God for those who will love and obey him.

What God treasures above all things in this earth, is his word. The word of God, although shrouded in mystery, it is the ultimate in creative power when activated by our faith. God's word is a treasure worth obtaining because it retains its value over time, even throughout eternity. Jesus said that heaven and earth may pass away, but the word of God will not pass away.[3] Here is a descriptive quote from Isaiah 55:10-11, *"As the rain and the snow comes down from heaven and does not return, but it waters the earth so that it buds and flourishes, so shall my word that goes forth from my mouth. It shall not return to me void, but it shall accomplish what I please and prosper in the thing for which I have sent it."* So no matter what happens in this earth, the Lord guarantees us that his word will come to pass and it will cause things in this earth to

1   Psalm 37:4
2   Deuteronomy 29:29
3   Matthew 24:35

flourish and prosper. Here is an added benefit. The psalmist David said that God's word is backed by the reputation of God's name.[4] Whatever God speaks to his people carries the full weight of God's presence, just as if God was speaking to us face to face. God doesn't have to show up to solve an issue on earth. He just has to send his word by his spirit and it will heal, deliver and prosper a people.[5]There was a Centurion with a sick servant. Jesus offered to come to heal the servant, but the Centurion interrupted by saying that he was not worthy that Jesus should come to his home. Instead, he requested that Jesus *speak the word only*. This Centurion was so confident in the value of Jesus' word that he knew that just by speaking the word, it (the word) would accomplish healing in the life of his servant.[6]

There is nothing wrong with having earthly treasure, but Jesus said that it is the fool who lays up treasure for him self instead of gaining treasure in God.[7] In the New Testament the word treasure is interpreted as the Greek word *thesauros*,[8] which means treasury or treasure store, a place where valuables are collected and stored. Any valuable thing is also considered treasure by this definition. This is the same word used for Roget's Thesaurus.[9] Perhaps Roget, a scientist and theologian, got the idea of treasuring words from the value he gained in studying the words of the Bible. You don't have to be a theologian to recognize that words are valuable treasure. Words shape our lives. They establish our view of life. Words can motivate us. They can also cripple and demoralize us as human beings. With words we bless or curse; love or hate our selves and others. Words get their value based upon the importance we place upon them. In fact this is how we value all earthy treasure. The object has no value except for that which our words, or the words of others have placed upon them. Every directive of our lives is based upon the words we have chosen to believe. Therefore, true treasure is not what we possess, but it is that which possesses and captivates our

---

4   Psalm 138:2
5   Psalm 107:20
6   Matthews 8:5-10
7   Luke 12:13-21
8   Blue Letter Bible. "Dictionary and Word Search for thēsauros (Strong's 2344)". Blue Letter Bible. 1996-2013. 18 Mar 2013. < http:// www.blueletterbible.org/lang/lexicon/lexicon.cfm? Strongs=G2344&t=KJV >
9   "Peter Mark Roget." Wikipedia, the Free Encyclopedia. N.p., n.d. Web. 18 Mar. 2013. <http://en.wikipedia.org/wiki/Peter_Mark_Roget>.

hearts and imaginations. True treasure begins in the heart, and manifests in our lives. It may begin as a sentiment, an attitude or an opinion, but when it takes hold of our hearts, it motivates us to action. We live out our destinies based upon the words we have chosen to believe, both the good and the evil.

Jesus taught us that whatever is in our hearts will be manifested in our lives. He said that out of the good treasure of a good man's heart, he would produce good things. Likewise, out of the evil treasure of an evil man's heart, he would produce evil things in this world. Jesus said that this happens because a man speaks from the abundance of what is in his heart.[10] Words come out of the abundance of that which we treasure in our hearts. If you want to know what is in someone's heart, just listen to the words he or she speaks. These same words can become the defining pattern of their lives. There are those who speak words to flatter and deceive, but like all men, it's what's in their hearts that identifies their true treasure.[11] If we want a more prosperous life, then we must find prosperous words and placed them in the treasury of our hearts. That's where God's words come into play. Every word that God speaks is designed to prosper our lives. When we meditate on God's words and we endeavor to bring them to pass, there will be successful and notable changes in our lives.[12]

God's words are spirit and life.[13] That means they are supernaturally life sustaining and prosperous. God's word offers a dimension of infallibility and stability that can withstand the test of time. It is impervious to social and financial instability. Therefore, true treasure can be found in seeking and enjoying the benefits God's word. God's word offers creativity, hope and promise in this world, and yet most American Christians have failed to recognize its value. This results from a lack of understanding of the word (the gospel) about God's kingdom purpose in this earth. Perhaps the confusion is because Jesus told us to lay up treasures in heaven and not in the earth.[14] Some may have interpreted this to mean that there is nothing of value in the earth and the only treasure worth retaining is that

---

10   Luke 6:45
11   Proverbs 23:6-7
12   Joshua 1:8
13   John 6:63
14   Matthew 6:19-21

which is in heaven; but God doesn't see the world as we see it.[15] In addition to treasuring his word, God loves and cherishes his human creation. He loved us so much that He sent Jesus to redeem us from the darkness of this world.[16] Jesus died and resurrected for us. Jesus endured the suffering on the cross because he saw the treasure that would result in our lives. He forever lives and makes intercession for us in order to extract the treasure from us that glorifies God.[17] He saw so much treasure on earth that he gave all that he had . . . He left his throne in heaven, came to this wicked earth, and gave his life so that the glorious treasure could be manifested in us. What is this treasure and where is it found? To answer these questions we have to start with the Holy Spirit of God.

The Holy Spirit is deposited in the hearts of everyone who receives Jesus Christ as Lord and Savior. The Holy Spirit communicates to us God's plan and purpose for our lives. Therefore the true treasure of God's kingdom is the revealed word of God, known as revelation knowledge of the kingdom that is placed within the hearts of men. This is the "kingdom within us,[18] the treasure in earthen vessels."[19] Eyes have not seen, nor have our ears heard, neither has it entered in the hearts of men what God has planned for our good in this earth.[20] It can only be revealed by the spirit. This is the Garden of Eden placed inside of us.[21] It is the glory of God placed inside of humans and revealed in the earth. This is "the manifested word" just like Jesus was the word manifested in the flesh,[22] and when we obey like Jesus obeyed, our lives also become the word manifested in this earth.

As followers of Jesus Christ we are called to be imitators of our creator God who saw lack, void and disorder in the earth and called forth from his spirit all of the creation we see today, including man.[23] Jesus said that rivers of living waters would flow out of our bellies. This is great treasure, the glory of God placed in men and revealed on earth as it springs forth out of our inner most beings with all the power of creation. This power is

---

15	Isaiah 55:8-9
16	John 3:16
17	Hebrews 7:20-25
18	Luke 17:21
19	II Corinthians 4:7
20	I Corinthians 2:9-10
21	Genesis 2:8-15; Isaiah 51:3
22	John 1:14
23	Genesis Chapters 1 and 2

manifested not only in healing and deliverance, but also in ideas, schemes and witty inventions that will reproduce the results of Eden in this earth. Whatever is lacking and void of order will suddenly produce all the wealth, beauty, abundance and order that heaven originally designed for our good.

Beloved, if you don't know God or his plan for your life, now is the time to seek him with all your heart. We are in a season that has never existed in the history of the world. For all who would dare believe God, he will lead you to immense treasures that will satisfy the longings of our soul and prosper you in health and wealth beyond human imagination. This is coming from someone who has found the treasure and keeps going back for more. If what you have heard has not whet your appetite for God's treasure, then keep reading. In the next chapter I share some highlights from my last adventure.

My Adventure To Eden

Did you ever wonder what happened to the Garden of Eden after Adam and Eve? So did I, until the Lord began talking to me about his glory manifesting in the lives of men on earth. He said that this glory was Eden. My spirit began crying out to God to lay hold of everything that he has for my life. I could hear it in my sleep. I wanted to lay hold of that for which Jesus laid hold of me. This had been going on for months. One day I heard the voice of the Lord say, "PAULA BE!" Then he gave me a vision that astounded me.

In the vision I was carrying a heavy royal mantel along with a crown and a scepter. I laid those things down and began bathing in what seemed to be a murky pool. The vision zoomed out and I saw that the murky pool was a pool of blood at the bottom of a hill that extended from the foot of the cross where Jesus had been crucified. I kept dunking myself in the pool when the Lord appeared. At this point in the vision and I found myself at a place in the spirit where several dimensions in time had intersected. The Lord was standing with me in the pool, and yet I looked up the hill and I could see his feet nailed to the cross and the blood was still alive and it was streaming down upon us. Then the Lord immersed me in the pool. It seemed like I was being baptized in that pool of blood at the bottom of the hill at the foot of the cross. When I came up out of the pool, the Lord began wringing out my hair. He was standing besides me and I noticed that he had to fully extend his right arm and turned to use his left hand to wring out my hair. When the Lord let my hair go, it landed at its full length in the center of my back. The Lord placed the crown on my head and helped me put on my mantel. He placed the scepter in my right hand and he grabbed my left hand and we began walking out of the pool alongside the bottom of the hill, but behind where the cross was extended. I didn't know where we were going there were only rocks and no exits. Then the Lord moved forward only a few steps from the pool of blood, and a portal appeared. I saw a golden sky, beautiful trees and meadows that seemed to appear from out of nowhere. It was then that I realized how grey and sullen the atmosphere was at the pool.

This place thru the portal was beautiful! When the Lord and I stepped through the portal, our clothes had also changed. We were both wearing a white robe and a golden crown. We were holding hands, running and laughing like two little children. The Lord said, "You did it! Welcome to the Kingdom!" This was it! This was the Garden of Eden that Adam saw. "That's all I had to do?" "That was easy," I replied. The Lord said, "Now, go and tell the others and invite them to come here as well." The vision ended as I basked in the splendor of the kingdom knowing that I had bridged the gap between heaven and earth; between time and space; and I had entered into a dimension where God's purpose intersected with my desire. This was Eden.

So, was this an actual place on the earth? I don't know. I do know that when I surrendered all that I had at the cross and asked to receive all that Jesus had for me, I found myself bathing in a pool of his blood beneath the hill where the cross still resides. Eden's portal was located only a few steps away from the pool, somewhere just beyond the cross. I had come to the place IN HIM where there were no barriers and no limits. This was the place where ALL THINGS ARE POSSIBLE and where everyone is invited come. Beloved, the Lord gave his life to prove his love for us. He resurrected with power so that we could be partakers of his new life in the Kingdom of God here on earth, not just in heaven. When we seek first the kingdom and endeavor to bring our part of the kingdom treasure to pass, this is our fellowship with the Lord, our partnership in the mystery of his suffering. Has God placed a desire within your heart? Whatever it is, it will lead to your treasure in the kingdom. Meditate on that desire and let the Holy Spirit help you bring it to pass in your life. Then take that desire and all that God has placed within you, and lay it at the foot of the cross. Surrender your will and lay hold of everything God has for you so that you might know HIM, and the power of his resurrection and the joyous treasures he provided for us through his sufferings on the cross. This is the inheritance that Adam lost. It is now available to all who dare to believe in Jesus Christ. This is Eden.

The Treasure Hunt Begins Now!

(Turn The Page)

Follow The Instructions
On
The Treasure Map

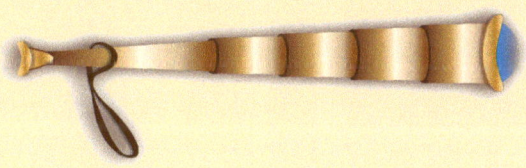

STEP 1
You Must Be BORN AGAIN

Page 39

✞T·R·E·A·S·U·R·E

STEP 4
Whatever HE Says,
DO IT! Page 59

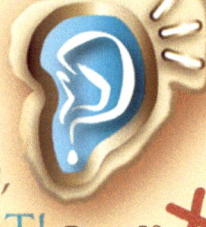

STEP 5
BEWARE
of Serpents, Wolves, Fool's Gold & Other Traps

Page 69

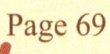

STEP 6
Go And Take
POSSESSION
Page 79

STEP 1:
You Must Be
BORN-AGAIN
(Reconciliation)

We've been talking about the kingdom treasure within us. Now we want to turn our attention to the first step in making this treasure a reality; bridging the gap between God and man in reconciliation. To do this, you must be born again.

From a kingdom point of view the spirit of man is key obtaining all the treasures of God. When we talk about the spirit, we are referring to the heart of a man; the place where the course of our lives is determined (Proverbs 4:23). The spirit (heart) of a man is where are the secret things are hidden from plain view. It is place where we are most authentic in our views about ourselves and the world around us. It is also the place where we tend to hide our most evil thoughts and plans. So often Christians will do something against the will of God and then say, "He knows my heart." This implies that the heart was right even if the action taken or words spoken were dead wrong. Some call it "keeping it real." I prefer to use the term "keeping it honest," or true to your heart, but just because you are true to your heart doesn't make you right in God's eyes. According to God, the human heart is deceitful above all things and it is desperately wicked (Jeremiah 17:9). God knows because he is the one who searches our hearts. The secret things belong to God; even the secrets of the human heart.

God has promised that he will judge each of us by the things that we say and do and by the secrets we hold in our hearts. From God's perspective, what's going on in the heart is <u>only</u> real, honest and true when it comes from him. Some people may be offended by that statement. You must remember that from heaven's vantage point, we are all fallen men; heirs of the curse that Adam propagated in this earth. Remember our paradigm shift? Forget about how you think or how you were taught according to the world. To obtain your treasure you have to be able to see the world as God sees it, then you must be willing to speak and act accordingly. This is the essence of faith. Have faith in God, not in the thoughts of this world or that from your past. You must desire a new purpose and a new direction for your life; one that God destined for you before the foundation of the world (Romans 8:28-30). You were born a tripartite being (body, soul, spirit) like God, now you must be conformed back into the image of God. The first step in that process was being born again, but without the Holy Spirit you cannot fulfill the will of God that conforms you into that image. In God's original plan, man was created in perfection. God formed him in his image and likeness and placed within man His Spirit, and man became a living, speaking spirit like God. At creation man was like God. Adam performed on earth, what God did in heaven. Adam spoke on earth, what God spoke in heaven. The son imitated the father. The father and son were of one mind and soul. Adam was commanded to be *fruitful and multiply.* This multiplication of sons was to continue throughout the earth. Today, God is still looking for sons; men, women and children who are willing to become true imitators of God in the earth. They will walk and talk like God. They will see that which is evil and corrupt, and speak that which their father wills. Supernatural transformation will replenish the earth with everlasting goodness and abundance.

Are ready to become a son of God? John 1:12 says that *"as many as received him (Jesus), to them gave he power to become the sons of God, even to them that believe on his name: Which were born, not of blood, nor of the will of the flesh, nor of the will of man, but of God."* Jesus came demonstrating what a son of God looks like in the earth. He also showed us the way. Jesus said, *"Verily, verily, I say unto thee, Except a man be born again, he cannot see the Kingdom of God (John 3:3)."* He also said that unless a man is born of water and of the spirit he cannot enter into the Kingdom of God (John 3:5). People so often take the born again experience very lightly. Christians think that it is about going to heaven and missing hell. No! It's about making a space in the human heart for God to reside like he did in Adam. It's a process of restoration; restoring humans back into the place of Blessing, prosperity and dominion. It requires that we remove the deceit and wickedness from our hears and make room for the Kingdom of God and all its mysterious treasures.

When Jesus came preaching the kingdom, a new era in human existence began. The evils hearts of men have been recalled to God's factory for the expressed purposes of installing of new (regenerated) hearts. These factory authorized hearts come with a kingdom guarantee. It's called a covenant; a covenant of the heart that does away with religion and superficial worship of God. The prophet Jeremiah prophesied about a covenant that would be written on the hearts of God's people (Jeremiah 31:31-34). Doesn't this sound familiar? The purpose of this book is to seek after a treasure in earthen vessels and to bring forth the kingdom within us; the script is written on our hearts by the Holy Spirit. Now do you get it? In order for the treasure to be placed within, you must have the regenerated heart. It's the only heart specimen that is designed to send and receive communication from God. Without this heart you can neither perceive nor can you enter into God's kingdom.

The regeneration process occurs when one is born of God's spirit. We call it being *born again*. The process is quite simple, and it begins with hearing the word about God's kingdom promises. Even while you are reading through this book the light of God's word should be entering into your heart and causing an "ah ha" moment, or a fluttering in your heart. For others it may be a complete transformation. How much light is shed into our hearts is specific to the individual. We will talk more about the anatomy of the heart in another chapter. For now, it is important to know that the unfolding of God's word always brings enlightenment and gives simple understanding (Psalm 119:130). It's a supernatural process that is quite subtle. The work of imparting understanding is done by the Holy Spirit (In the next chapter we will talk more about the role and responsibility of the Holy Spirit in our covenant).

There are many ways to describe the regeneration process. The Bible talks about begin washed with water of the word (Ephesians 5:26). There is a supernatural cleansing of the heart and mind that occurs when the word of the kingdom enters into the heart. At the same time, while the cleansing is going on, the Holy Spirit comes to reside in your heart. Remember how Adam lost the kingdom and was thrown out of the garden? It happened when he lost the spiritual oneness with God because of sin. When Adam decided that he no longer wanted to follow God, the Holy Spirit was removed from his being. Adam was left as a shell of the man that he was at creation. For the first time, man had become a carnal being who was no longer led by the Spirit of God. From that time until now, humans have had to develop their own sense knowledge and intellect to be able to survive on their own in this vast world. That was not God's original plan. This was the heritage of the curse that Adam left all human kind as a legacy. Humans were no longer connected to God's Spirit and were left with hearts void of the life and breath of God. They were from that moment on, born dead to God. To receive God's treasure, one must be reconnected to the life of God through the spirit. We call this *regeneration*. Others call it recreation, but the idea is the same. The heart is returned to its pristine state, and liken to that which was placed within Adam at creation. In fact, it is exactly the same process that occurred for all creation. Stay with me for one moment while I explain. If you can get this explanation, then you will have taken hold of one of the most powerful keys in God's kingdom operation.

Let's go back to Genesis 1:1-3. God created the heavens and earth, but he did so while the earth was in an evil state, *"And the earth was without form, and void; and darkness was upon the face of the deep."* Now, doesn't this sound like the condition of the human heart that is disorderly, empty and dark? Watch what happens next at creation, *"And the Spirit of God moved (hovered) upon the face of the waters."* Why was the Spirit of God brooding over the earth? This implies that God was affectionately and loving anticipating that something great was about to happen; that something marvelous was to come forth from this dark, empty mass. Perhaps it was a diamond in the ruff, or some other treasure hidden in darkness. Hidden treasure . . . get it? Beloved, God sees our darkened hearts just like he saw the darkened earth that day at creation. Yes, it was ugly and evil, but God saw the treasure and spoke words of life that transformed the earth into a beautiful paradise; a paradise that was the glory and reflection of heaven itself. So when God said, *"Let there be light,"* the Holy Spirit swung into action and brought light forth, out that which was steeped in darkness. Now, if God can do that with this huge planet, imagine what he can do within the heart of one man.

God is not moved by darkness covering the earth, nor is he moved by the gross darkness that overtakes the hearts of men. God only sees the possibilities of treasure placed within you; true treasure that changes the world (Isaiah 60:1-3). All it takes is for the sons of God to imitate their father and bring forth their father's will (treasure) to pass in the earth. So, I ask again. Are you ready to become a son of God? We said that Jesus left us with an example of how to live like sons of God in this earth. What did he do? Jesus said and did only what his father said, and what he saw his father do. Remember, this is how you live out the image and likeness of God. This is how you become an imitator of God like dear children (Ephesians 5:1). This is also how Adam lived until he decided to abandon the plan of God to do his own thing. Perhaps you are a born again Christian who erred like Adam by deciding to do your own thing. God promised us a place (in him) where we would experience days of heaven upon the earth: a day of rest for the people of God, where we would cease from doing our own works and the rest in the completed work that Jesus completed on the cross when he said, *"It is finished."* If you want to obtain the treasure within you, then repent now. Turn your heart back to God, open your eyes to see his plan and open your ear to hear his voice, and follow his instructions from now on.

If you have **never** been born again you can do so now as well. You might have heard people talk about salvation or getting saved. It's all part of being born again. You will be saved from the curse and the spiritual death and destruction it brings. In addition, you will inherit all the blessings of God, and eternal life that begins here on earth; and one day you will go to heaven and be with God forever. Again, the plan of salvation is the same thing worded slightly differently. It means throwing off the evil curse and taking on all the wonderful benefits of God's kingdom. Why so many different ways to say the same thing? In this book I explain things from the kingdom perspective beginning with Adam and ending with Jesus. That is how the Lord commanded me to teach. My job is to teach the kingdom. Jesus also taught the kingdom, but to a slightly different audience. He taught in ways that Jews under the covenant of Abraham could understand. He taught from the Old Testament prophets and attempted to bring people to the New Testament view of life. In general the church in America teaches anything but what Jesus taught. Very few even comprehend how salvation fits within God's kingdom plan for the world. Basically salvation means being rescued from the curse, but it also means being placed into the kingdom where all the good things in Eden are once again available to men on earth. As we said before, this was all made possible by Jesus' death and resurrection. Our covenant was secured with the blood that Jesus shed on the cross, therefore it is a blood covenant. Which provided a way for sin to be washed and the Holy Spirit to renew our spirits. You are being asked to walk away from the life of your past and to exchange it for a new life under this blood covenant. You are also being asked to live like Jesus lived on the earth, as a son of God; to make him your master and Lord.

The Bible is filled with covenant promises. In this book, we'll show you how to activate things under the covenant with the help of the Holy Spirit. We will also show you what it takes to become an imitator (son) of God. Remember how God spoke at creation and the earth went from darkness to light? The same can be true for you today. With a few simple words you will be delivered from the power of darkness and translated into the Kingdom of God's dear son (Colossians 1:13). You won't necessarily look or feel different, but there will be a noticeable difference in your spirit. Your heart will be changed. You'll know it because the Holy Spirit will supernaturally deposit the love of God into your heart (Romans 5:5). You will begin sensing things on a higher spiritual level than ever before. You will also have an unusual hunger and thirst for spiritual things pertaining to God's kingdom. You'll be like a newborn babe, desiring more and more of the one who gives and sustains your life. Your sustenance **is** the word of God. If you are ready to take this life transforming process, just pray this simple prayer out loud.

Dear God,
I want to be a partaker of the new life that Jesus made possible in the blood covenant. I no longer desire to do my own thing, but desire to bring forth that great treasure you have planned for my life. Wash me from my sin, renew my spirit with Your Holy Spirit. Lead me, teach me and guide me and I will follow you all the days of my life.
In Jesus Name I pray. Amen.

If you prayed the prayer above. Congratulations! You are now a member of the family of God, and heirs of the kingdom. You should do the following on a daily basis:
1. Spend time reading the Bible and talking to your father. Let him tell you of the glorious treasures that await you.
2. Whatever he speaks, meditate on that word day and night so that you can make your way prosperous and have good success.
3. Enjoy your new birth and endeavor to walk in it every day.

Also, find a good church that teaches the Bible and believes in the Holy Spirit. Which brings us to the next step that will empower you to obtain your treasure.

STEP 2:

Be Filled With
THE HOLY SPIRIT
(Empowerment)

In the last chapter we mentioned both the blood covenant and the role and responsibilities of the Holy Spirit. Now we will put them both together in detail. The major thing to note is that the blood covenant is very much alive and active more than two thousand years after Jesus' death and resurrection. The Holy Spirit called it a ***"Covenant partnership."*** Where everything we have belongs to God and everything he has belongs to us. Each of us agrees to perform certain duties under this covenant arrangement. Jesus agreed to suffer and die, our part of the agreement is to walk in the newness of life that was provided in his death and resurrection. The Holy Spirit is the advocate who executes the agreement.

You may remember that my vision of Eden identified the supernatural connection between the cross, the covenant and the Garden of Eden. The cross is a symbol of the blood covenant and the Garden of Eden is the manifestation of God's kingdom and his blessing in the earth. American Christianity teaches the cross as a symbol of the pain, suffering and death of Jesus, but the cross represents so much more than payment for our sin. The Lord called the cross ***"a portal into God's Kingdom that has the ability to impart both the power and wisdom of God, to transform any and every situation on this earth."*** That means that the cross has supernatural powers that can transform this world. This is the power of the Holy Spirit. Remember that the Holy Spirit is a person. He is the God the Holy Ghost. At salvation the full power of Holy Spirit comes to reside inside the heart of every believer. So, if you prayed the prayer of salvation in the last chapter, *God is living inside of you.*

Think about that. The same God that created the earth is hovering inside of your heart in earnest expectation of something marvelous to happen in your life. This is explosive Holy Ghost power. It is the same power that raised Jesus from the dead, and it is residing inside of you. If the Holy Spirit could raise Jesus from the dead, just know that he can do the same for every dead and dying situation in and around you (Romans

8:11). With the power of God working for us, nothing is impossible. Ephesians 3:20 says that God is able to do *exceeding abundantly above everything we can ask or think*, **but** it is according to the power of God that is working in us. So if you want great transformation in your life, it is necessary to let the Holy Spirit have full reign over every situation you face.

The Holy Spirit is our assistant and guide. He is the *parakletos* or legal advocate of our blood covenant. The Holy Spirit is like an executor of God's will for our new lives in the kingdom. He has access to the sealed documents with our names on it. He has access to all that belongs to God in heaven. His job is to relay to our spirits **all** that belongs to us. He also has the power necessary to bring those things to pass in our lives. When we said that our treasure was written on our hearts by the Holy Spirit, we need to know that he also has the power to bring it to pass when we obey his instructions. This is a portion of our covenant that is sealed in a mystery. None of this would be possible if it hadn't been for the blood covenant. This power has granted us access to our rightful inheritance in God's Kingdom. We prophesied that God was restoring this **"ancient dynasty"** that was established at creation. The cross is also our portal of transformation into that dynasty. If it weren't for the cross, we'd have no access to God, or to the things of God and his kingdom. Now, we who are in the family of God, are joint heirs with Jesus to all that belongs to the father. The Holy Spirit is our legal executor of that inheritance.

Now that we have discussed the covenant and the power of the cross we need to know how to tap into that power and make it work in our every day lives. What I am about to say causes much confusion in the church because there are so many pastors teaching against the Holy Spirit. Truth is; *If you want what God has for your life, you must be born again and filled with the Holy Spirit.* As we discussed the Holy Spirit is key to unlocking God's power and wisdom in your life. At salvation the Holy Spirit is deposited in our hearts, but he will not do anything without our permission. He has to be released and placed in activation. Even after you are filled, the Holy Spirit won't do anything unless you ask him to do it for you. He works for us; but if you don't employ him, he'll stand around and wait until you call upon him. In fact, the Lord never revealed my purpose it until I became filled with the spirit with the evidence of speaking in tongues. Again there are denominations that teach against tongues. They don't understand that speaking in tongues releases the power and wisdom through the Holy Spirit. Tongues unlocks mysteries (I Corinthians 14:2) concerning your situation on earth. There also times that we don't know how to pray or what to pray (Romans 8:26). That's when the Holy Spirit uses our tongues to converse with God in our heavenly language. There have been times in my life when a problem existed that seemed insurmountable. After just a few moments of praying in tongues, that thing was solved. I even remember being so oppressed that I was unable to pray. When I opened my mouth to pray in tongues a groan came up out of my spirit. There was a supernatural power released through my spirit. I didn't need to know what was happening in the spirit, I just needed to know that power was made available in the spirit to break me free. Again, when we speak in tongues we are speaking mysteries to God about our situation on earth. Praying in tongues also keeps us from operating in our fleshly emotions, desires and lusts of the flesh. Instead we build ourselves up on our most holy faith by speaking in tongues (Jude 1:20). In the next chapter we will take a closer look at the fleshly things hinder the power of the Holy Spirit from working in our lives.

Here is one last piece of advice about working with the Holy Spirit. The Holy Spirit has a legal obligation to execute our covenant, therefore he will not violate the laws of God for any reason. If you desire a legal remedy, he will not respond to an emotional appeal. He only answers when we come to him in spirit and in truth of God's word. This is God's law. If you don't know the word, tell him the issue and ask the Holy Spirit to direct you a *"legal code"* that applies in your situation. There are many Christians who will kick, scream, cry and spit hoping that God will do something to help them. If you did that sort of thing in front of an attorney he may have you thrown out of his office. The Holy Spirit will just ignore you, which is also why many people don't get answers to their prayers. Another reason people don't their prayers answered is because they are routinely disobedient. If you make it a habit of ignoring the instructions of the Holy Spirit, he will stop speaking until you begin to obey the last thing he told you to do. Also, if you stop operating in love and become deceitful, disrespectful or dishonorable to God or to his people, the Holy Spirit will attempt to correct you, but if you ignore him, he will also ignore you. The goal of the Holy Spirit is to help you manifest the kingdom and complete your race lawfully (II Timothy 2:5). He is a supernatural being who holds great weight in the kingdom. He desires to teach you whatever you need to know to obtain that treasure which God has reserved you. He wants you to succeed in all you attempt to do. Make the Holy Spirit your close friend and ally and you will be walking in signs and wonders and nothing will be impossible for you.

Want to be filled with the Holy Spirit right now?
Pray this short prayer out loud.

Dear Father in Heaven,
Thank you for sending Jesus to make a way for us to walk in the power and wisdom of your kingdom. Fill me with your Holy Spirit so that I can tap into that wisdom and power for my life. I also want to obtain the treasure you have laid up for me. Holy Spirit be my comforter and guide daily. Lead me along that perfect path day by day. I receive my gift of tongues. Teach me how to pray in full faith and power of the kingdom. In Jesus' Name I pray. Amen.

Here are some additional scriptures that will help you learn more about the benefit of speaking in tongues and other spiritual gifts.

The Holy Spirit and Tongues

John 4:14	Acts 1:8
John 7:38	Acts 2:1-4, 38
John 14:16-17, 26	Acts 4:8
John 15:26-27	Acts 8:14-17
John 16:7-15	Acts 19:1-6

Spiritual Gifts and Fruit (Evidence) of the Holy Spirit
I Corinthians Chapters 12, 13, 14
Galatians 5:22-23
Ephesians 5:9

STEP 3:

Yield Your Members To RIGHTEOUSNESS
(Surrendering)

Now that you are born again and filled with the Holy Spirit, there is something you need to know. *Even though you have a new desire for the things of God, the desire for sin may still be present in your life.* Do not be alarmed. If you prayed the prayer with an honest and sincere heart, you **were delivered** from the power of darkness and translated into the kingdom of God. The angels of the Lord are rejoicing at your decision, but demons are angry and they will try to get you back into their kingdom. This is spiritual warfare. Do not fear. This is also not the time to be discouraged. It's time to suit up and run to the battle to defend your decision for Christ. Rely on the Comforter (the Holy Spirit). He will teach your hands to war.

Before salvation you were outside of the kingdom with no hope. Now, as heir of God and joint heir with Jesus Christ, you have a mighty arsenal available to you. The beauty of living in God's kingdom is that we have a choice to live for God and not for sin. A sinner has no choice, and until he or she is regenerated, they have no capacity to live for God. The ability to live for God is one of the miracles of the cross. It made supernatural power available so that each day we can live out the words, *"but as for me and my house, we will serve the LORD (Joshua 24:15)."* Most people use this verse to refer to their family, but God showed me how to use it in referring to the *whole human being; body, soul and spirit*. These are our members. Together they make up our human house. For the power of God to work efficiently on our behalf, our entire house (body, soul and spirit) has to be in agreement with God. A house divided cannot stand in power (Matthews 12:25), it will fall (Luke 11:17). During regeneration human spirit is changed, but the soul and body must be brought under submission. Most people think this as an impossible feat, but conceptually it is easier than you can think.

The Lord compares the process to that which an Olympic athlete endures to win the gold. There is extensive physical training, but there is also mental strengthening and spiritual alignment so that the whole being is programmed to be a champion. You may have heard of athletes using visualization techniques to over come their fears and weaknesses. They also study the strength and weakness of their competitors. So, for an athlete to be fit to run and win the race, it takes conditioning of the whole being. The same is true for one who desires to obtain great treasure in God's kingdom. The Apostle Paul talked about running the race to win the prize. To do so, the body must be brought under and made subject to the spirit that is aligned with God (I Corinthians 9:24-27). We don't do this alone. The Holy Spirit is our manager and trainer who is commissioned to guide us to success. If you want to obtain your treasure there may be times when you must command your house to love and obey God. Don't be surprised by this. The Holy Spirit knows what's out of line and remember that he is the one steering you to the treasure, so obey him.

I have just shared what he Lord taught me, but this is not the norm for most Christians. Many have no power because they still do not understand how important it is for us to present our bodies as a living sacrifice to God. This is what God expects. We are also commanded to no longer conform to the world's way of operating, but to renew our minds with how God and his kingdom operates. In addition, we need to evaluate ourselves by God's measurements and not by our own (Romans 12:1-3). Let's go back to the example of the athlete. What would happen if one day the athlete (who had never run a race) decided that he was unbeatable and decided to fire his trainer and refused to train? This would be considered foolishness because one can only know his or her true abilities during competition with others, and yet this is how many in the church operate. There are many Christians who believe that once they become saved that they are flawless; believing that everything they say and do has been approved by God. Wrong! Salvation need happen only once, but sanctification (cleansing for God's service) is an ongoing process.

Believers should be growing up in the things of God, and at each new level of growth there is a grooming that takes place. There are habits and things we must release so that we can obtain that which the Lord has for us. We are part of a covenant partnership. Jesus did his part and we are also expected to do our part. Still, there are many deceived souls who will never complete the destiny God has for them because they are satisfied to live defeated in this world. They long for a place in heaven, but they dishonor God with their lack of concern about being holy as He is holy. These are unclean vessels that serve as poor witnesses to the overcoming power of God's kingdom.

Years ago I was visiting the home of a friend who had offered me a refreshing beverage. We were standing in her dimly lit kitchen when she opened the dishwasher to get a glass. As she picked up the glass, I saw what looked like red lipstick on the rim of the glass. I politely told her that the glass was not clean, and she began to argue with me. *Of course the glass was clean, she just took it out of the dishwasher, right?* Well, my friend was highly insulted by my remark so I flipped on the light switch so that she could clearly see the glass. Not only did it have the thick red lipstick stain, but also at the bottom of the glass there was sediment from all the other dirty dishes. My friend was embarrassed by this incident, but the Lord used this situation to make a point about Christians. He said that many think that since they went through the salvation cycle that they are perfectly clean. This is usually where they end the process, but they need to turn on the light of the word to see clearly.

The Lord explained that when his power flows through such an unclean vessel, that the sediment would rise to the top and anyone following such a person would also be defiled with the same filth. Unfortunately, God's people have been under the leadership of men and women who have unclean vessels. That is why there is so much sin and no power in the church. The Body of Christ is divided in its members; individually and as a whole. Remember that a house divided cannot stand. So where does the defilement come from? It comes from the things that we see with our eyes, what we hear with our ears and what we value in our hearts. Defilement comes from the secrets we hide in our hearts. Things like: evil thoughts, adulteries, fornications, murders, thefts, covetousness, wickedness, deceit, lasciviousness, an evil eye, blasphemy, pride, and foolishness (Mark 7:14-23). This is why the Bible tells us to guard our hearts with vigilance (Proverbs 4:23). There are many things that can enter the heart and prevent the Holy Spirit from operating in your life.

Remember that our covenant is written on our hearts, but if we also have junk from our past, lies from the enemy and other things in our hearts, they will compete against power of the Holy Spirit that is in us. Again, God is able to do exceeding abundantly above all we can ask or think

according to the power that works in you (Ephesians 3:20). If God's supernatural power is not working in your life, let's take a look at what may be siphoning off that power. Below is a diagram of the human heart that the Lord gave me over fifteen years ago after I questioned why there was little or no power operating in the lives of spirit-filled Christians. The Lord revealed idolatry; worshipping something other than God. It is a sin against God, and yet it is very common in the church. The Lord said that although the Holy Spirit may be inside of their hearts, he had little room to operate because they valued others things more than the things of God. Jesus quoted Isaiah when confronting the church of his day, *"This people draweth nigh unto me with their mouth, and honoureth me with their lips; but their heart is far from me (Matthew 15:8)."*

Take a look at the diagram below. These are types of things that people value more than God. These things hinder God's power in your life. Could there be things in your heart that are taking precedence over the Holy Spirit in you? The Bible says that a divided heart (double-minded) is unstable in all it's ways. It will receive nothing from the Lord (James 1:5-8), and yet this is how many Christians live. What's the solution?

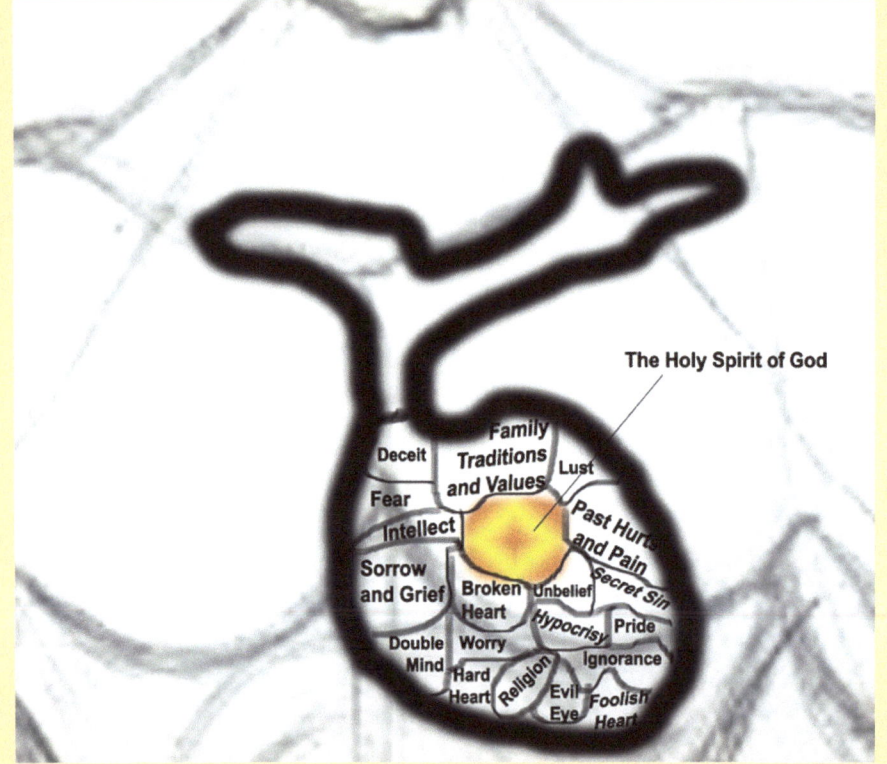

First of all, repent. Change your mind and your ways. We need to clean our minds and hearts and become singularly focused on what God wants for our lives. This means we must also forgive, because if we don't forgive, God won't forgive us (Matthew 6:15). No forgiveness; no power.

When you sin, don't hide it, confess it and God will be faithful to forgive and cleanse you (I John 1:9). Jesus died for your sorrow and our grief (Isaiah 53:4) so let it go. Continue washing your mind and heart with the word of God (Ephesians 5:26). God's word is truth. His truth will make you free. Pray also that the words of your mouth and the meditations of your heart are acceptable to God (Psalm 19:14) and let the Holy Spirit help you get there. Endeavor to walk like Jesus walked then you will abide in him and produce much fruit for the kingdom (I John 2:6). Let's look at an example.

Suppose you have read something on the web, watched something on television or heard a story on the news and it begins to take hold of your mind. You have power to stop it dead in it's tracks. We are commanded to cast down all imaginations and anything that exalts itself against the knowledge of God. We are to capture every thought and bring it into obedience to God (II Corinthians 10:5). You may say, "I can't control my thoughts." Sure you can! God would never command us to do something without giving us the power to do it. Remember, you have the mind of Christ. Use it! You have the Blood of Jesus that cleanses your conscience from all dead works so that you can serve the living God (Hebrews 9:14). Plead the Blood over your mind and your thoughts and over anything that tries to hinder the work of God in your life. It may take a bit of practice, but you can do it. You **must** do it if you want to obtain and enjoy your treasure. Let the Holy Spirit help you. He was sent to help us with our infirmities (Romans 8:26). These are our weaknesses and frailties. The Holy Spirit is our intercessor. He not only prays for us, but he relays information about our weaknesses and shows us how to overcome them. He is our Helper. Let him help you! And by all means pray in tongues to build up the power in your spirit.

That's how we deal with the evil that attacks our thoughts. Also keep in mind, that we walk by faith and not by fear. If we value something more than we value God, it is because we have more faith in that thing than we do in God. We trust that thing to give us what we want because we fear that God won't. For a Christian to operate in such a manner is a display of genuine hypocrisy. If this is the condition or your heart, you are seriously at war with God. Repent and get back on track with God. Here is what Apostle James had to say about such behavior (James 4:1-10). This is "The Message" version, *"Where do you think all these appalling wars and quarrels come from? Do you think they just happen? Think again. They come about because you want your own way, and fight for it deep inside yourselves. You lust for what you don't have and are willing to kill to get it. You want what isn't yours and will risk violence to get your hands on it. You wouldn't think of just asking God for it, would you? And why not? Because you know you'd be asking for what you have no right to. You're spoiled children, each wanting your own way. You're cheating on God. If all you want is your own way, flirting with the world every chance you get, you end up enemies of God and his way. And do you suppose God doesn't care? The proverb has it that "he's a fiercely jealous lover." And what he gives in love is far better than anything else you'll find. It's common knowledge that "God goes against the willful proud; God gives grace to the willing humble." So let God work his will in you. Yell a loud no to the Devil and watch him scamper. Say a quiet yes to God and he'll be there in no time. Quit dabbling in sin. Purify your inner life. Quit playing the field. Hit bottom, and cry your eyes out. The fun and games are over. Get serious, really serious. Get down on your knees before the Master; it's the only way you'll get on your feet."* There you have it, a cleverly spoken diagnosis and solution to the issue of a divided heart; which by the way is also called an *adulterous heart* in the King James Version of the Bible.

Now I want to turn my attention to two final issues of the mind that the Lord brought to my attention. The Lord said that because Americans are heavily into entertainment, Internet porn and social media issues are flourishing amongst his people and they need to be addressed. One is *narcissism* and the other *is vain (evil) imaginations*. There is a reason that these types of things are appealing to the masses. They appeal to the lowest form of human desires, *lust*. Lust is a trap for humans because they think since it's natural, that it is also good. No! Quite the opposite is true. Remember that human nature is operating from the curse that Adam left us. Therefore, what seems natural to us is abnormal and evil to God, simply because he never created us to do those things. He created us to ascend to glorious heights of rulership; but if you can't rule your own body or mind, you are not fit to rule the world. Americans have also learned how to succeed in corruption. Therefore financial success or fame from corruption becomes an incentive for others to follow. We now have generations of people who view corruption as normal. It's a twisted way of operating that eventually falls apart because there are spiritual laws in the unseen realm that govern what happens in the earth.

Men will always reap what they have sown. Evil and corrupt seeds always produce evil and corrupt harvests. Take a look at *narcissism,* which combines vanity, ignorance and pride. This occurs when people are so self absorbed in their own importance that it's like they are staring at themselves in a mirror in admiration of their own beauty. This happens so easily on the Internet as people base their importance on how many people clicked the "like button" on their social media page, or how many friends they have on their page. In most cases, the people don't know enough about the real person to either like or to be their real friend. People conceal themselves behind social media while others bear it all; the good, the bad, and oh, so much ugly . . . and how proud they are to spew their garbage viral. People arise to popularity because of self-debasing expressions and debauchery. What's trending on the web is often rumor, filth or sensationalism, and those who rank the highest most often have an inflated perception of their own achievements.

The sad thing about narcissism is that it traps its victims in an endless cycle of make believe and failure. They have very low self-esteems and thrive on the validation of others, but the validation is not based on a true assessment of their potential or success in life. Until they look beyond the web statistics as the sum measure of success, they won't be motivated to move into greater depths of life. In other words, they will never seek God's treasure because they think they **are** the treasure all in themselves.

Ecclesiastes 11:4 says that those who watch the wind will never sow anything, and he who stares at the clouds will never reap. People are often crippled in life because of their twisted thoughts. They will never accomplish anything of value. They are stuck in the lowest place of human existence because of the meditations of their hearts. Internet porn is a prime example. Rather than living and loving in real life, these people are stuck in a fleeting fantasy that will never come to pass in their lives. They are so detached from reality, that if they have a spouse and family, they are treated like inanimate objects while the person in their fantasy is treated as though he or she were real.

When the Lord began showing me this type of imagination many years ago, he likened to the women I knew who were hooked on soap operas. They watched daily, the lives of the soap opera characters that appeared more real and exciting than people in their own lives. These women began detaching from their families and slipping into fantasies that would never be fulfilled. I witnessed the same thing with Christian women who were hooked on romance novels that filled their heads with fantasy. I watched as these women aborted the treasure God had for them, if the man God sent didn't look or act like those in their fantasies. Americans also tend to erect idols of television, film and music personalities. *IDOLS!* These are people we imagine to be gods because of their popularity of their success in the world. Yet, they are not gods at all. God is a jealous god! He said that if we created and worshipped anyone or thing above him, he would curse us to the third and fourth generation (Exodus 20:5). God didn't lie, he means this wholeheartedly.

The imagination is a powerful tool given to us by God, but anytime we decide to use it to make a name for ourselves or to exalt the evil desires of our hearts, it makes God jealous and he will come in and disrupt things. He did it with the Tower of Babel when the people were in agreement in their evil imaginations (Genesis 11:1-9). The same is happening in America's political, economic and religious systems. The corrupted fantasy of the American dream is in the process of falling apart. The dream was once real, but we corrupted it. Now there is new leadership fighting against the reigning giant of corruption, and as we said earlier in this book God is vowing to take down the billionaires who have brought this nation to its ruin.

So, why did God give us our mind and imagination? God desired that we would use our minds and imaginations to meditate on his word and his will for your life. There are giants to slay and nations to rescue from poverty and oppression. There are also mighty adversaries who lie in wait to oppose our every move. To win, we need all our faculties about us, and we need to hear the instruction of the Lord. That way if he tells you that by your hands the walls of Jericho are going to fall, you can put that in your imagination, and stand up to the challenge. Meditate on that word day and night. Visualize it and put it into your memory. See that thing done because according to heaven *it is finished*. Then you would have made your way prosperous and have good success (Joshua 1:8).

This is how the God kind of faith works. It takes some work, but after a while you will get the hang of it; and when you get the treasure, you'll realized that it was all worth the effort. Again, do not fear and don't be discouraged. Be strong and courageous (Joshua 1:7). Be anxious for nothing, but in everything by prayer and supplication, with thanksgiving, let your requests be made known to God; and the peace of God will guard your mind and heart. Finally, whatsoever things are true, whatsoever things are honest, whatsoever things are just, whatsoever things are pure, whatsoever things are lovely, whatsoever things are of good report; if there be any virtue, and if there be any praise, think and meditate on these things (Philippians 4:6-8).

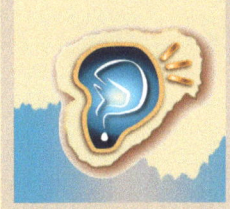

STEP 4:

Whatever HE Says,
DO IT!
(Hearing)

This chapter is on faith (hearing and obeying). Faith is both our weapon and our shield. It is the single most important thing in God's kingdom, because without faith, it is impossible to please God (Hebrews 11:6). Faith requires that we are both actively attentive and responsive to the instructions of the Holy Spirit. We'll also learn that there are some key components to faith; mainly that of love, which works very closely with honor and patience (or endurance).

Let's begin by defining faith. The Bible tells us that faith is the substance of things you hope for, it is the evidence of things not yet seen (Hebrews 11:1). Faith is not hope, but it involves hope. Faith is not wishful thinking or an empty expectation. Faith is so real that it is a living force of action. Many call it the *currency* of heaven. Currency implies an active and living mechanism that creates and sustains life. Here is the definition the Holy Spirit gave to me.

"Faith is:
- ***A conviction that is so strong that you just know in your knower that what you are hearing is true.***
- ***A spiritual force that moves not only the heart of God, but the force of faith also moves nature and the laws of this universe.***
- ***Designed to produce specific results that affect multiple lives and multiple circumstances simultaneously.***
- ***Like a guided missile whose target is to eliminate lack and bring prosperity. It will bring increase that will multiply and replenish the earth.***

Where there is faith, there will be glory and the plan and purpose of God manifested in the earth. This is the faith of God."

That definition came directly from heaven. Now that we know what it is, where does faith originate? How do we obtain faith?

The Bible tells us that faith comes from God. In fact, it is God's faith that he gives to us. Let's go back to the idea of faith being like currency.

If faith were a check from heaven, God would write it in our name and give it to us expecting us to cash it in at the bank. Unfortunately, there are a lot of checks from heaven that were never cashed because God's people didn't recognized that *it was* money in the bank. They seem to have watered faith down to grabbing a scripture and rubbing it on God's belly to make it come to pass *someday*. There is nothing magical about faith. We simply take what God gives us and give it back to him. That's how simple faith can be. It amounts to doing and saying whatever he tells us to do and say, and yet God's people do and say whatever they want then complain when God does not respond to their request.

Let's go back to the check example. It is written to a specific person in a specific amount. You can't take it to the bank and demand that they give you a car instead of cash. You can't demand that they give you twice as much as it was written on the check. It is what it was when God sent the check from heaven. This is the legal tender of heaven. Cash the check and get on with it! If you want what God has, you have to do things his way. He makes the rules.

We said that faith comes from God. How does he distribute it to us? When one comes into the kingdom, God distributes to each person a measure of faith (Romans 12:3). What that measure is precisely, God only knows for sure. We do know that each person is given the same faith, in the same measure. Again this is God's faith that we are expected to use and bring its fruit back to the kingdom. Where is this faith? It resides within our hearts. When the Holy Spirit comes inside of your heart, he brings with him the faith of God. I might also mention that the Holy Spirit also with him the love of God. Just like we had to activate the Holy Spirit by receiving him, the same is true with the love of God. One must receive the love of God in order be able to walk in faith. As we said, faith works by love. This is important to know because religious Christians sometimes bash unbelievers for not obeying God. You cannot force someone to obey God if the love and faith of God is not in them. They have no capacity to obey God until their hearts have been regenerated. Even then, one must receive what God offers before it can show up in their lives.

So let's tie this all together with your hunt for treasure. The Holy Spirit writes the script on our hearts. Along with this script comes the faith (and love) to get the job done. We not only get the script which is the thing God desires for us to do in the earth, but he give us the currency (faith)to get it done. Faith brings all with it all the necessary resources to get God's plan manifested in the earth. All we have to do is to exercise our faith in God. If we believe him, then we will do what God says so we can have what he says we can have. We mentioned that faith works by love. There is another reason this is important to know? For one, God is love (I John 4:8), and our faith can only work **through** him. Secondly, Jesus commanded us to love; to love God and to love our neighbor. Love is the greatest commandment (Matthew 22:37-40). Jesus also said that if we loved him we would obey him (John 14:23). So our obedience shows that we love him. Without love, we just go through the motions without changing according to God's original plan. We could have faith enough to move mountains, but if we don't have love, its a waste of time and serves only as an outer appearance (I Corinthians 13:2). Love, real (God's) love goes to the core of an issue and it changes the very fabric of one's being. God's love never fails (I Corinthians 13:8). We also mentioned that love and honor go hand in hand. We are commanded to esteem others higher than ourselves (Philippians 2:3). We are to honor all men, especially those who have authority over us. We must love the brethren, fear God and honor the king and all governmental rulers (I Peter 2:17). Avoid offense at all cost. Give the battle to God and stay focused on obtaining that true treasure that awaits you.

We have just seen how faith and love work together, but let us look at where patience or endurance plays a key role. This is also where we learn how to use faith as both a weapon and a shield. This is spiritual warfare. The Apostle James says to count it all joy when you fall into various trials. Trials? Yes! Your faith will be tested. How else would you know that faith works. Trials and heats are necessary in athletic competitions. The same is true with faith, especially if you want to obtain your treasure, and there will be many treasures available during your lifetime. In this season, the Lord said we had to be like *"Olympic athletes in the spirit."* This will be by far, the most exciting part of your adventure. The testing of your faith will produce endurance. Remember your measure of faith? Think of it like a muscle, a *faith muscle*. The more it is exercised the stronger and more "buffed" you get. This is the result of enduring the trials. James says to let patience have its perfect work, so that you may be perfect, complete and lacking nothing (James 1:1-4). Are you ready to start a brief training exercise? Let's get started. I will share spiritual techniques the Lord has taught me in addition going over important scriptures you should also know. Let's put what we've learned so far, in an active warfare situation. *Now that you have gotten all this information and motivation, the enemy will exert pressure in an attempt to make you give up what you've just learned. This will be a full on assault. What do you do?* Panicking and running is not an option. You face the challenge just like it came to you; *full on assault*, but we do it God's way. The best defense is to submit yourself to God. Ask the Holy Spirit to give you the best tactic in this situation. Then do whatever he says to do and stay focused. Don't let the enemy throw you off focus. If the enemy does begin to attack by throwing up dust or sending hindering nuisances your way, ignore him unless the Holy Spirit tells you otherwise. Take this as a compliment. It means that the enemy knows he has no power over you. Distraction is his only defense. Just remember that the same power that raised Jesus from the dead is residing in you. You must rely on God's power only. **Submit yourself to God, then you will have both the power and authority to resist the devil. As a son of God you already have the authority, but only when you are obedient will you also be able to acquire the raw power to win.** That's why you must obey God. This is not a flesh and blood war. Physical tactics will not work. Only God's weapons will win in the spirit realm.

We are told to submit to God, resist the devil and he will flee (James 4:7). On your own, you have no authority to resist the devil. We are strong only in the Lord and in the power of his might. Remember that! And, the devil will eventually flee . . . but only for a season (Luke 4:13). Beloved, as long as you are on this earth the devil will come after you. That's his job. God has an everlasting love for you, but Satan has an everlasting hatred towards you. Stay in the love of God and you will always win against the devil, no matter how many times he comes back to threaten you. He has no teeth! He has a loud roar, yes, but no teeth. Jesus broke out all of his teeth. That's the power of the cross.

We've talked about being strong in the Lord, now let's put on the whole armor of God (Ephesians 6:10-18). The word of God is our weapon and our shield. Hey wait a minute. Didn't we say that faith was both our weapon and shield? So, what is the real deal here? The word of God is full of the faith of God. In our prophetic definition of faith, the Lord said that faith was *"like a guided missile."* There are many components to a missile. I'm no ballistics expert, but I can imagine that there is an outer casing that serves as a container for a more powerful combination of combustible substances that set off a chemical reaction either on impact or upon detonation. Given that, imagine that God's word is the outer casing and faith is the substance (no pun intended) inside the container. How about that. So when the Holy Spirit writes a script upon our hearts. It's like a loaded missile waiting for us to launch with our faith. It is when our faith connects with God's faith, which is encapsulated inside of the word, that detonation takes places! Wow! Faith can be downright explosive. In fact, there are times in spirit-filled church services when a prophetic word goes forth, it may feel like an explosive was set off in your spirit. That's why people will start screaming and running around. With the treasure within you, now the explosive will detonate your spirit even if you're not in church. Let me give you a personal example.

Early one Sunday morning the Holy Spirit directed me to go to a local coffee shop to write a message to post for the web that day. I have a favorite table with lamps and it looks more like a seat in a library. While busy taking dictation from the Holy Spirit, a man asked if he could sit at the end of that same table. Understand that the word of the Lord was not being spoken with my mouth, it was being released from my spirit as I wrote on my laptop. As I wrote, the Holy Spirit began moving upon me. Every time the Holy Spirit surged, this man would jump in his seat. The more I wrote, the greater the Holy Spirit moved upon me; and the more the man jumped. I pretended not to notice his reaction while trying to stay focused on what the Lord was saying to me. After I finished writing I apologized for the disruption and let him know that kind of thing always happens when I write prophetically. While speaking, the Lord gave me a prophesy for this man. Not only did he receive the word, he was amazed that it was about a project he was working on that very moment. He kept repeating what I said, and he thanked me. Now, that's how active and powerful the word of God can be, especially when we are obedient to the Holy Spirit. Notice that in this one instance, we proved our prophetic definition of faith. The word I was writing went to the online target audience like a guided missile, but it also caused change in the life of a bystander who was on his way somewhere else.

Here it is again. According to our definition faith is *"like a guided missile"* which means it has a specific target *"to eliminate lack and bring prosperity; to affect multiple lives and multiple circumstances simultaneously. It will bring increase that will multiply and replenish the earth."* If this could happen with one person's obedience, just image what could happen if all of us were obeying the Holy Spirit collectively. This is why obtaining your treasure is so important. It is designed to change the world with simple acts of obedience. To be totally armed to take on the devil you must also be armed with the word on *truth, righteousness, peace, faith and salvation.* Don't be as concerned about whether you have on a helmet, a belt or a breast plate as much as you should know that each part of the armor represents a particular aspect of the word of God. I say this because many have used this scripture to preach that there is no armor for our rear. First of all, when the Apostle Paul spoke about the armor, he was talking to ancient people in symbols they understood. To imply that the armory of God has nothing but ancient armor for our day of modern warfare is preposterous! The Bible never said that we had no protection from the rear, in fact it clearly says quite the opposite. It says that the Lord is our rear guard (Isaiah 58:8). The Lord was a cloud by day and a fire by night for the children of Israel in the wilderness to protect them from the Egyptians (Exodus 14:19). The grace and favor of the Lord surround us like a shield (Psalm 5:12). Psalm 91:11 says that his angels are given command to keep us on all our ways. That includes our front and rear. Psalm 121:7-8 says that the Lord shall keep us from all evil! He shall keep us whether we are going out or coming in. That alone should let you know that God is watching your back.

As a new believer don't always believe what people teach, let the Holy Spirit confirm the word and by all means open your own Bible and read it for yourselves. The more word you know, the more ammunition will have to defeat the devil. Also faith comes by hearing, and hearing by the word of God (Romans 10:17). Remember faith is a muscle. The more you hear, the more you feed your faith. As you hear more, you can expect to be tried and proven even more. Work those faith muscles. You are training to become a spiritual Olympian.

Here are some common enemy tactics to look for. *The devil will try to undermine the word you have heard from God.* The enemy will try to tempt you like he did Eve in the Garden. If God said that you are going to be wealthy, the Devil will ask, "Did God say you would be wealthy?" Then he will attack your finances in ways to destroy your faith in what God said. If God says that your marriage or your virtue would be your greatest asset to the kingdom. Again the enemy will say, "So, I thought you were so honorable and virtuous. If you were what God said none of this evil would be happening to you." This is how the enemy will hit you. Jesus went through this as well. Right after he was baptized and the Holy Ghost appeared like a dove, there was a voice heard from heaven saying (Matthew 3:16), *"This is my beloved son in whom I am well pleased."* All of the earth heard these words (which means all the demons heard it too). Immediately the Holy Spirit leads Jesus into the wilderness to be tempted of the devil. Read Matthew Chapter 4 and it will show you how Jesus dealt with his new call in God. He had to war with the devil, and the first thing that the devil said was, *"If you be the son of God."* He heard what God said. The devil wanted to see if Jesus actually believed what he heard. If he did it to Jesus, he will do the same to you. Another the key strategy to remember is this. *Whatever the devil questions in your life is the very place where your power lies in the kingdom.* This is where your armor comes into play. Suit up for battle everyday, knowing that you have already won in the spirit, you just have to walk it out in this physical realm. Don't' let the devil cheat you out of God's will for your life. Through Christ you are more than a conqueror (Romans 8:37). Present your members for service as an undivided house and renew the mind with the word of God (Romans 12:1-2). Do the will of the Lord from the heart (Ephesians 6:6). Follow after righteousness (1 Timothy 6:11) and let the grace and favor of God carry you to your destiny in Christ.

Your goal is to obtain the treasure God has stored up for you with the agility and prowess of an Olympian. Most Christians never get to this point in the faith because of a defeated slave mentality. They have settled for leeks and onions and the slavery scenarios of Egypt. The treasure is in the Promised Land. If that is your destination you must be diligent to yield your members to do and stay on that path without being deceived by those who have no desire to enter in and possess the land. They are trembling over the giants in the land. Beloved, let me say it again, the power that raised Jesus from the dead resides within you. What is a little giant to the Almighty God within you? Stay focused on the treasure, but be armed with the *truth*. God's word is *truth* (John 17:17). The word on *righteousness* is straightforward and goes hand in hand with *salvation*. When you received Jesus as Lord, you became the righteousness of God (II Corinthians 5:21). This means that Jesus took your sin and gave you his right standing with God. You are accepted in the beloved family of God. If you happen to sin today or tomorrow, that condition doesn't change. You simply repent and get back in line with God's plan for your life. Don't let the devil trick you into thinking that because you are not perfect, you never were really saved. None of us are perfect. The perfection comes from a loving father who made a way for us to receive an abundance of his grace and the free gift of righteousness so that we could reign over the enemy in this life by one Christ Jesus (Romans 5:17). We cannot reign by our power, only in his power. It the love of God that perfects us. When we fully receive that love it will cast out any fears (I John 4:18) the enemy might raise concerning our security in Christ. We were once enemies of God and children of wrath, but when we chose salvation, we were reconciled back to God. We now have peace through the Blood of Jesus. He is our peace (Ephesians 2:14). Stay close to the Holy Spirit and he will give you the faith to stand on in a battle. Don't be shocked if some of the enemy's tactics come from family, friends, coworkers, even ministers and pastors. The enemy will use anyone to battle against you. He likes to use those you least expect because it causes the greatest blow to your faith. Don't let them offend you. These people don't know what they are doing. The devil is using them. Have faith in God, not in your circumstances, not in what other's say or do. If you want to obtain your treasure you must believe God above all other voices in this world. We walk by faith and not by what we see (II Corinthians 5:7). We don't even judge a situation by what others speak in our ears. We operate with the eyes and ears of faith.

Finally, I want to talk about the sword of the spirit. This is the *rhema* word of God. It is probably the greatest weapon in the Lord's arsenal because it brings swift action against the enemy. Faith is now; it is alive and immediate. It's not something we make up on our own. It comes from the Holy as right now word that is spoken to our spirits. Sometimes that *rhema* word may instruct you to do something rather odd, like go dip in the muddy water seven times, or pour water into a pitcher to produce wine. How about the ten lepers who were told to go show themselves to the priest and they hadn't yet been healed? It was against Jewish law for lepers to be among the congregation and yet Jesus sent them to the priest. When the ten headed toward the temple, they were healed. God is a rewarder of faith. We prove our faith by obeying what we have heard. The miracle is always in our obedience. Whatever he says do; do it, no matter how strange or odd it seems. Get your head out of it. This is a spiritual transaction. God uses the foolish things of this world to confound the wisdom of men (I Corinthians 1:27). Here is an example of what I mean.

The Lord had me working with a minister in a particular city. God set this woman up for miracle after miracle. He would ask me what I wanted for lunch. I would respond by telling him what I wanted to eat. The Lord would always tell me to go look in Dee's cabinets and you will find what you are looking for. Dee didn't work outside of the home and she didn't have much money to grocery shop, but every time I went to her cabinets I'd find the food I wanted. It became well known that food was appearing in Dee's cabinets. People began coming over with grocery sacks and filling them up with food that Dee never bought, and to this day we don't know how it got in those cabinets. In any case, Dee was feeding people in her neighborhood from her cabinets. This had gone on for weeks.

One day, Dee called me complaining that she needed some money. While she was complaining, the Lord had me tell her that all the money she needed was in her apartment. In fact, the Lord kept showing me a huge jug filled with coins. She said that had only pennies but the Lord showed me that there were bills inside of that jug. Dee began to argue that she knew what was in that jug because she was the one who put the coins in there. Well, I knew what God told me, so I hung up the phone and drove to her apartment. I went to where the Lord said the jug was in her apartment and I told her to get me a wire clothes hanger. I bent the hanger so I could reach into the jar and the minute I put the hanger inside the jar, bills appeared in the midst of the coins. Were they there before I got there or after I obeyed God? I really didn't care. All I knew was that the bills were in the jar and I kept pulling them out and placing them on Dee's table. She began crying at the miracle that was happening before her eyes. She asked, "Where did all this money come from?" I answered, "The same place where that food came from that kept appearing in your cabinets." And the word of the Lord came to me and he told her how he had demonstrated his love and care by supernaturally providing for her. God loves us that much, but he is looking for faith.

Several months later the Lord had us spread this miracle working power to everyone we knew. He told us that whatever we asked in prayer, he would grant. So she and I decided to call everyone we knew and we asked for their greatest need; and true to his word, God answered every prayer just like he said he would. Cancers were cured, crack heads became sober and in their right minds, marriages were restored. Why does God do this? He wants us to know that he is alive and well able to supply our every need. All he asks if for a little faith from us; even mustard seed faith would work; and he would do exceeding abundantly above all we could ask or think. Keep you ears open to hear the will of God for you. Keep your heart in the ready to receive mode. Then whatever he says do, do it!

STEP 5:
BEWARE
Of Serpents, Wolves, Fool's Gold & Other Traps
(Discernment)

The closer you come to your treasure, the more clever the enemy tactics. The enemy will come to you in a more fierce and cunning way. He won't necessary appear as an enemy, but more like a friendly confident or advisor. It may be someone close to you, or even a complete stranger claiming to be an expert in the area of your pursuit. At first glance this person may seem to be genuinely interested in helping you, but know that underneath that smooth exterior is the devil's advocate who is trying to see what you know in order to overthrow your pursuit and steal your treasure. They want it for themselves. These are predators that you will find along the way to your treasure. There will also be that which looks much like your treasure, but a closer look proves that it's nothing more than a hoax. If you haven't figured it out yet, our topic in this chapter happens to be that of deception. You will need discernment to identify and conquer deception.

Before we present the deceivers it is best that we expose the truth about what God is doing in the earth and just how crucial your treasure is in this hour. What is most exciting about God's treasure is that it is *apostolic* in nature. This term is used in referring to the first apostles, but it also applies to those whom God sends out as messengers and emissaries. We are in the last days, and the Lord has unusual projects and missions to accomplish before Jesus returns. God is sending out messengers, but they are not in the form of street corner preachers of yesteryears. He has chosen apostles in business and industry. These are the innovators and entrepreneurs of these last days. God is boldly sending people in uncharted territories to do an amazing new work; something that has never been done before. God wants to show how a world economy should be run according to kingdom principles. It will be a glimpse of how things will be run when Jesus takes his rightful throne here on earth. This is a difficult message for many Christians because they have been taught that you get saved and go to heaven. They never paid attention to the message of the kingdom that Jesus taught.

When the Lord called me, he told me that I would teach what Jesus taught: the kingdom. He had his disciples to pray *"Thy kingdom come, thy will be done on earth as it is done in heaven* (Matthew 6:10).*"* At the beginning of this book we presented a prophecy where God said he was about to restore his kingdom dynasty in the earth. That is consistent with what Jesus said. So if the kingdom is coming to earth, why are Christians trying to get to heaven? They have been deceived into believing that treasures are only in heaven. We also want to make sure you are not deceived about where your treasure is stored.

The treasures have been reserved for us by heaven, but they are for release here in this earth. This takes us back to the example about the check from the heaven. As children of God, there is an account reserved for each of us in the Bank of Heaven. Our Father gives us his faith like a bank check written in our name. What we do with that check determines how much we have in our personal account to draw upon in this earth. We are also ambassadors for the kingdom, which means that all of our provision comes from the kingdom, but it is for us to use while on assignment on the earth. In addition, everything in the kingdom works on the principle of seedtime and harvest. Our obedience is sown in this earth and we receive a harvest of treasure in our heavenly accounts for use on earth. Have you ever been away on business for a company that paid your expenses? The idea is similar. If you travel continually, the company will give you a certain monthly allowance. It behooves you to use all that is given. If it appears that it's more than you need, your allowance could be downsized, but on the other hand, if it appears that the allowance is not sufficient to cover your expanded scope of business, the company will consider giving more to meet the need (if the funds are available). In God's kingdom, there is never a shortage of funds, only a shortage of faithful stewards. Why would he increase the treasure in your account if you have never used what you were given in the first place?

Jesus explained this principle in the parable of the talents (Matthew 25:14-30). He said that the kingdom of God operates like this. There was a man who was headed on a journey, but before he left he divided money amongst his servants according to their ability to make a profit. To one he gave five talents. To another he gave two and another he gave on talent. The man left on his journey. Both the one with five and the one with two talents doubled their Lord's money, but he who had one talent dug a hole in the ground and buried his Lord's money. When the man returned from his journey and found the two servants had doubled his money, he was joyful and said, *"Well done, good and faithful servant; thou hast been faithful over a few things, I will make thee ruler over many things: enter thou into the joy of thy lord."* The man was angry at the servant who buried the money, when he could have put the money in the bank and earned interest. He took the one talent from this servant and gave it to the one who had ten. Here is the principle in summary: *"For unto every one that hath shall be given, and he shall have abundance: but from him that hath not shall be taken away even that which he hath. And cast ye the unprofitable servant into outer darkness: there shall be weeping and gnashing of teeth."* This particular scripture is repeated five times in the Bible and it is used in three different parables. So it must be an important note about the kingdom, and indeed it is. The Kingdom of God is a kingdom of increase. Citizens of this kingdom are expected to produce a profit. Jesus said (John 15:5), *"I am the vine, ye are the branches: He that abideth in me, and I in him, the same bringeth forth much fruit: for without me ye can do nothing. if a man abide not in me, he is cast forth as a branch, and is withered; and men gather them, and cast them into the fire, and they are burned."* This is a bold and serious statement coming from Jesus. The message is clear. Those who are faithful with what God gave them will be given more in abundance, and he will take from the unfaithful and give it to one he can trust. Woe to the unfaithful man for there is also punishment awaiting him.

Now, you who dare to pursue your treasure in this hour are on the road to becoming a *"good and faithful servant."* Most of the church has no clue that there is treasure awaiting them in this life. They are also unaware that they will be judged for that which was allotted to them in the kingdom. Therefore, God will bless you abundantly for your faithfulness for two reasons: 1) you are embarking upon an adventure that the church deems impossible, 2) not only is it possible, but also these treasures are enormous feats designed to make up for where the church has feared to go. You will be like David who dared to slay Goliath while God's people trembled in fear. The treasures that many of you obtain will be of this apostolic nature. Don't be overwhelmed. We serve a bold God who is looking for us to represent him boldly in this earth. There is much to be done in the kingdom and little time left before Jesus returns. God is about to get bold and radical in these last days. Don't be surprised at what he has designated for you in this hour. It is both great and glorious. For a great effectual door has opened to you, **and** there are many adversaries (I Corinthians 16:9). Do you have what it takes to get the job done? Of course you do. It resides within you. Remember how we said that the script written on your heart is loaded with an explosive faith missile? God created you in his likeness and his image. You are now reconnected to God's power source in the Holy Spirit. There is now, nothing that is impossible for you. Be an imitator of your father in heaven. There is a supernatural hero inside of you that is waiting to be released. This hero will transform the world. This is Christ in you, the hope of glory (Colossians 1:27).

There you have it! That was a glimpse of the truth of what you are about to obtain. As I mentioned, there are many adversaries. Don't be surprise by the level of hatred and deception that is about to come your way. Most of the issues will be with the church. There will be much jealousy because you will do in the public sector what they failed to do in their congregations. You will demonstrate the kingdom, not religion, not church, but the power of God's kingdom dynasty. This makes you a triple treat to many in the church. At the same time there are those who are hungering for more of what God has, but they have been discouraged by the church. Once you emerge with your treasure, these delighted souls will also be motivated to hunt for their own treasure. There will also be others in the world who will think that you have lost your mind. They will ridicule you once they find out that you are doing something far out and different. Even Goliath had disdain for David (I Samuel 17:42), but it made no difference in the outcome. David still took Goliath's head. We said it before and will say it again. God uses foolish things to prove his superiority over the wisdom of men (I Corinthians 1:27). Let them laugh. Just you remain faithful, and in the end, you and the heavenly host will have the last laugh.

Let's take a closer look at these adversaries. Earlier in this book we alluded to the serpent who beguiled Eve in the Garden. *Serpents* are more subtle than any other creature (Genesis 3:1). They will attempt to throw you off track by getting you to take your eyes off of God's treasure and focusing on your lower human instincts. You may find that they even hide in the grass and in the trees along your path, carefully observing your every move. They surface at the moment they sense you are tired, frustrated, or otherwise not at the top of your game. They entice you with what looks good, what feels good and what strokes your ego and pride. Serpents pretend to offer you relief from the struggle that God puts you through. They pretend to sympathize with you, but in their hearts they want you to give up and quit. These tend to be people who had the same opportunity you had, but they couldn't make the cut. If they can't have the treasure, they don't want you to have it either. Avoid serpents by walking by faith (whatever God says) and you won't be tempted to fulfill the lust of your flesh. Then there are the *wolves*. Jesus warned us that there would be false prophets he called wolves dressed in sheep's clothing (Matthew 7:15). Wolves are predators amongst us masquerading as believers in Jesus Christ. Basically, there are two types of wolves in the church, both are equally dangerous: 1) There are those who think they are hearing from God, but are not, and 2) Those who are pretending to hear from God. Regardless of what is going on in their heads, their hearts desire is the same. They both want to be seen as a spiritual authority in order to gain attention and popularity for themselves.

A false prophet will always draw people's attention away from God and on to themselves. They play god with other people's lives and it always leads to death. They don't believe in Jesus Christ, but they crave to be around those who do believe, only to slaughter them. Wolves have an insatiable appetite for blood and nothing satisfies them more than leading innocent sheep astray for the purpose of slaughtering them. Wolves can also be sadistic in nature, especially when one is suffering or hurt. Never take advice from a wolf because they are setting you up for the kill. They may tell you that they have a word for you from God. Don't believe it. Their mouths are full of lies. Those who think they are hearing from God are sometimes hard to detect because they come across as genuine, but they are being led by familiar spirits from the pit of hell. These wolves really believe that they are sheep, but they have never surrendered to God in order to be led by the Holy Spirit. Like all wolves, they tend to run in packs with those who are also deceivers. They are uncomfortable around those with are walking and talking with the full power of God. These wolves (false prophets) will label them as witches and false prophets. They are in the habit of calling that which is good, bad and calling that which is bad, good.

The more popular the wolf, the more dangerous they are to the congregation because people will believe the false prophet before they will believe the Bible or one who is sent by God. Whoever follows their advice will only find death; the death of their call and purpose; death of the anointing on their lives, and eventually physical death and eternal separation from God. Wolves can be very religious and self righteous. They never seem to come to the knowledge of the truth because in their hearts they are righteous and they are self motivated in all their ways. Most vicious wolves know that they are not sheep. They come amongst God's people only to mock God. Like all wolves, they want to appear spiritual and will be quick to give you their advice and tell you it was from God. They want to draw your blood. They hope you fall for their deception. These wolves will not only watch you fall, but they are notorious for denying responsibility after you have taken their advice. Some will laugh in your face for having believed them rather than obeying God. Others will even quote scripture to justify their religious stance against you. False prophets will judge and condemn all in the same breath, leaving the sheep cut up, stabbed and bleeding on the floor. The best way to avoid being destroyed by a wolf, is to confirm every prophetic word with the Bible and with the Holy Spirit. In the mouths of two or three witnesses the truth will be established (Matthew 18:16).

The last two adversaries we will discuss are not necessarily found in the Bible, but the Holy Spirit wanted me to include them in this chapter as well. We will talk about *prospectors*. The one thing about prospectors is that they are explorers. They are looking for precious treasure based upon what they have heard and research they have acquired, but they have no real evidence that treasure exists. On the other hand, if you are attempting to seek and enjoy the treasure God has for you, avoid prospectors at all cost. Most often it may be someone within the church who thinks he or she knows better how you should pursue that which God gave you. They may even be an expert in your field, but they don't have the wisdom nor the anointing of God to do things the way God has directed you. Prospectors want your treasure and they will place stumbling blocks and toss comments your way that imply that since others have failed at what you are doing, so will you. Some may even diminish the value of what God has given you by telling you that either it has already been done, that anybody can do what you are doing, or that someone is more qualified to do it than you. Deep down in their hearts, prospectors are jealous of what you have. If they could they would take it from you, instead they want to stop you from pursuing the treasure. Prospectors want to break your spirit and curb your ambition. When a prospector comes onto your path, you can politely listen to what they have to say, but when they have finished talking, only do what God told you to do.

Finally, there are the *claim jumpers* who are also closely watching your every move. They want to do the same thing you are doing, but they have somewhat of a conscience in that they won't pursue your treasure until they think you have abandoned it. If you abandon it, they will be quick to claim your treasure as their own and fight for their right to have it. After all, you didn't want it. Well, here is what you need to know about your treasure, others may think they can claim it and they may even try to take it from you, but if God didn't give it to them, it won't work. God's treasure has been designed specifically to highlight your personal background and your spiritual gifts. It is custom made only for you. So, what happens if we abandon our treasures? Will God give them to someone else? Let's look at Isaiah 55:10-11 again. *"For as the rain cometh down, and the snow from heaven, and returneth not thither, but watereth the earth, and maketh it bring forth and bud, that it may give seed to the sower, and bread to the eater: So shall my word be that goeth forth out of my mouth: it shall not return unto me void, but it shall accomplish that which I please, and it shall prosper [in the thing] whereto I sent it."* If God sent his word and the Holy Spirit wrote it upon your heart, it will come to pass in this earth. The word will accomplish what God pleases and it will prosper in the thing he has chosen. Now whether it comes to pass for you is another thing. If you choose not to carry out the assignment, just like we said earlier, the Lord will give it to someone more faithful, but it won't have the same flavor. It will be the same general thing, but tailored for another personality and gifting set.

Can a person go to God and petition to take up your treasure and manifest it in the earth? Sure they can. Again, whether or not God grants their request is another thing. Deuteronomy 29:29 says, *"The secret things belong unto the LORD our God: but those things which are revealed belong unto us and to our children for ever, that we may do all the words of this law."* The treasure within each of us comes in the form of a mystery. Once these secrets are revealed, they become our heritage; an inheritance to pass down through our family. Therefore God's treasure is ordained as an assignment for a particular family; a natural and/or spiritual family. If someone rejects the treasure, it is passed to the next qualified individual in that natural or spiritual family. The greatest example is King David. He desired to build a temple for the Lord, but God didn't allow him to do so because he was a man of war. God did promise David that his son Solomon would succeed him as king and would be qualified to build the temple in his stead (I Chronicles 28:2-10). In addition, the

Lord promised David that someone from his lineage would always be on the throne over Israel. When Solomon took the throne, the Lord told him that his sons could keep the throne as long as he remained a faithful son to God. Solomon became unfaithful when he took strange wives who served their own gods. They turned Solomon's heart away from the Lord. God told Solomon that his sons would not be king over Israel because of his sin. Instead the Lord promised to raise up Solomon's servant to be king. God chose Jeroboam as king over Israel. This caused such a rift that the nation split (I Kings 11). Part of the nation became Judah under the rule of Solomon's son Rehoboam. Jeroboam ruled over Israel. In doing so, God kept his promise to David, but it was not his blood son, but a servant son raised in his house that reigned as king.

You may also remember that when John the Baptist came preaching (Matthew 3:2, 8-9) *"repent for the kingdom of heaven is at hand,"* the Jewish leaders of that day felt that they were already in the kingdom and had no reason to repent. Their reasoning: they were children of Abraham. John said that God was able to raise children of Abraham from the stones. In other words, if they didn't want to obey to obtain their kingdom heritage, God would find someone else who would. Indeed he has. That is why Christians exist today. When the Jews rejected their Messiah, Jesus commanded the Apostles to take the kingdom to the world. The Jews were not eliminated from the promise all together. The Bible says that they will one day recognize Jesus as their Messiah, but in the meantime the gospel of the kingdom and all of its treasure is being extended to the entire world. So God can give your treasure to another if it fulfills his purpose and his word.

Now that we have talked about some of the adversaries you can expect along your course, there is one more area of deception you should watch out for: *fool's gold*. This happens when you find something that seems like treasure, but it is not the thing God prepared for you. On the surface it looks like the Garden of the Lord but it ends up being Sodom. That's what happened to Lot when he and Abraham parted ways (Genesis 13:8-13). Lot moved to a place that seemed to be a beautiful portion of land that was well-watered, but the men of the city were exceeding wicked sinners. Lot thought he was looking at the garden of the Lord. The Lord eventually had to rescue Lot and his family before raining down fire and brimstone on the cities of Sodom and Gomorrah (Genesis 19:15-26). It is common for people to mistake fool's gold for true treasure, **if** you are not being led by the Holy Spirit. In fact, most people in the world would see nothing wrong with seeing something and desiring to have it. It is not what we see that is the problem. It's when what we see becomes an unhealthy obsession. This is lust. Lust is covetousness, which is a sin. Again, in the world lust is accepted as normal, but in God's kingdom it is a deadly sin. Lust caused Eve to eat the forbidden fruit, which led Adam to do the same thing. They were thrown out of the garden and cursed because something caught their eye and turned their hearts away from the command of God. In a previous chapter we talked about the things in the heart that limit the power of the Holy Spirit in your life. Lust was identified in our diagram. Lust is an unlawful desire for something we want in this life. The desire may be natural, but how we go about it determines whether lust has taken place. Since natural desires come from God, he has a specified route for obtaining that which we desire. To fulfill that desire any other way is lust. Lust usually comes from something we have seen with our eyes. As mentioned earlier, one of the main entrances to heart is through our eyes. What captures the eye, can also capture the soul (mind, will and emotions). When we begin to meditate on something we've seen, it becomes imprinted upon our hearts and mind. Just looking at something doesn't make an impression. It's the meditation in the mind that leads straight to the heart of a man.

We should also mention that what we hear can also affect our minds and hearts. Again, hearing alone is not an issue. Hearing and meditating on what we have heard makes an impression on the mind and heart. And why not? We said that faith comes by hearing and meditating on the word of God. This makes a positive impression in the heart that will help lead us to our treasure. Also what we see with our eyes of faith also makes a positive impression on the heart. Our faith has eyes when the Holy Spirit unveils a mystery and speaks revelatory words and shows the details in a vision or dream. These are the type of impressions that will catapult us to manifest our treasure in the earth.

Fool's gold can manifest in may ways and it often looks, sounds and feels like true treasure, but something is amiss. If you don't stop and consider what is going on in the spirit, you could end up forfeiting your treasure and ending up with a counterfeit. Remember how we said that whatever God has ordained for you, the enemy will question your call. Well so often the enemy will do that by sending people and things in your life that ordinary people would "kill for" and people will even call you a fool for turning down such offers. They don't realize that it may look good for some people, but you are working toward your destiny and that requires you to operate at a higher level; God's kingdom level. God kingdom operates far above anything that the human mind could ever understand. When we obey the instructions of the Holy Spirit we will also find ourselves living a life that is also at a higher level.

Follow the Holy Spirit and he will help you discern that which is truth from the deception. Don't be swayed by what appeals to your secret desires, your senses or your ego, and you will find yourself at the highest level of success available to men on earth!

STEP 6:

Go And Take POSSESSION
(Reward)

You have overcome the obstacles along your course, the treasure is now within reach. It's time to go take possession. Tread lightly and gather your goods quickly and discreetly lest you stir the interest of nearby fortune hunters. Although you may conceal some of your booty for a short season, there will be a day when the Lord will tell you to put it on and walk in it proudly. This may be your treasure for all eternity, but it was never really about you. It was all about God's glory manifesting on your life.

The Bible is filled with epic stories about those who excelled in faith and obtained great victories in life, but too few of those stories are being demonstrated in our world today. It's not that God isn't able any more, it's because people's hearts have grown hard. They don't believe any more. The goodness and favor of God seem like fables and tall tales to even those who call themselves Christian. By successfully completing your hunt for treasure, you will have proven them all wrong. God is faithful to his word, if we would only be diligent and faithful to believe his word is true. II Chronicles 16:9 says that the eyes of the Lord run to and fro throughout the whole earth, to find someone whose heart is perfect towards him, just so that he can show himself strong on their behalf. God desperately wants to do us good in a major way, if we would only let him, and you beloved have made him proud this day. Now go and enjoy the fruits of your labor for this is truly a gift of God (Ecclesiastes 5:19).

Conclusion
Protecting Your Treasure From Pirates

Our final discussion is about pirates. The name "pirate" usually conjures up images of evil men overtaking ships and stealing valuable treasure. While that is true. There is more to pirating than meets the eye. The Holy Spirit said, ***"pirates want to deprive you of your liberty."*** They hate the fact that you have reached a level of success that they deem unobtainable for themselves. Jealousy and envy arises in their hearts against you, and while they may take your treasure, their true desire is to inflict fear as a way of constraining your achievements and reducing your personal power. Pirates are invaders who would raid and flay you if given the opportunity. They think they know you personally although they watch you from afar. Their victims are not chosen randomly. Pirates are always looking for the outward signs of wealth, power and esteem. They study their victims and make their attacks very personal.

Who are these pirates and where do they come from? Pirates can be complete strangers who target you because of your money or claim to fame; like ambulance chasers and people who throw themselves in front of your car, or those who stage an accident in your business or in your home for the purpose of suing you. These people will also threaten to kidnap your child and hold them for ransom. They may hijack your corporate shipments, rob your bank or hold your employees hostage. In America, there are pirates and bootleggers in almost any industry that is making enormous financial profits. They offer their goods underground in the black markets of the world. The message these pirates send to the original artist or manufacturer is this: *no matter how unique or popular your product, we can and will steal it from you.* Since piracy is profitable to some degree (until you get busted), it will continue to exist in the world economy. How do you deal with these pirates? Industry pirates work underground so until they surface there really isn't any way of finding them and prosecuting them in a court of law. However, since they are underground and they work in secret, they are playing right into the hands of God. Remember how we said that the secret things belong to God? That means **anything** that is done in secret, God will reveal publicly (Luke 12:2). God is the revealer of secrets (Daniel 2:47). In addition, the Lord has provided remedies in his kingdom for those who steal from us. If someone kidnaps your family member, sells and enslaves them, they shall receive death (Deuteronomy 24:7). If they steal your goods, and the thief is found, he must pay you back as much seven times more than what he stole, even to the value of his entire household (Proverbs 6:31). God will execute justice for all who will demand of him. Pirates beware! God has given us the keys to the kingdom. Whatever we bind on earth, God will bind in heaven (Matthew 16:19). We have the power to loose the angels of the Lord to expose the pirates and bind up their illegal activities forever.

Pirates could also be people you know. These are those who had some personal contact or relationship with you, either lasting or on the acquaintance level. They may also be long lost relatives begging for money, not because you owe them anything, but because they feel you should share your good fortune with them. After all you are family. Then there are the ex's: ex-spouses, ex-roommates, and ex-cons from your past who will step forward to make false claims against your treasure. How about women claiming you as the father of their child and you never knew the person on an intimate level? There may even be people who agreed to work with you on a project then they changed their minds and decided to have nothing to do with you or your "stupid" project. The minute that you are successful their tune changes and they think you owe them because they say you got the idea from them. If they can't prove their claim in court, they may show up publicly as a cheap imitation of you. They may even disrespect and dishonor you with rumors and lies to sway the public opinion against you. They think they are doing this to stop the press from glorifying you, but actually they are going against God and attempting to diminish the impact of his glory upon your life. Woe to the one who takes that which is good (from God) and labels it as evil (Isaiah 5:20). These are pirates and haters.

This last one is for all those who easily fall for flattery. If you were a physically ugly or unattractive person who repelled the opposite sex, and now that you have the treasure they are flocking to your side as if you are the most attractive thing on earth, here is a new flash. They are still not attracted to you. They are attracted to your anointing, your wealth or your fame, but it's definitely not you. They may even run after you wanting to get married, but it's not about you, it's about what you have that they can steal from you. These are the heartbreaking pirates that make fools of wealthy old men and women. Guard your heart and let God lead you to the one person who will be true to God and true to your heart no matter what you possess.

Finally, I want to leave you with an empowering Bible example of someone who found his treasure in God and fought through most of what we have discussed in this book. In fact we have used the example of David many times to explain how to seek and enjoy your treasure from God. This last example occurs when David is hidden in the land of the philistines and while he and his men are out winning battles, the Amalekites invade their homes in Ziglag, burn everything and take the women and children hostage (I Samuel 30). At a time when the men should have been greeted with loving cheers for their heroism, the enemy made sure they came home to defeat and anguish over their families. This was such a severe blow to these mighty men of valor that they threatened to stone David to death. He was their leader who led them to great victories and great spoils and now they had turned their pain and anger towards him. The Bible says that David was greatly distressed, but he encouraged himself in the Lord his God. David when into prayer and enquired of the Lord what he should do, *"Shall I pursue after this troop? Shall I overtake them?"* God answered him, *"Pursue: for thou shalt surely overtake them, and without fail recover all."*

The men were already exhausted from battle, but David was able to convince four hundred men to go with him to overtake the Amalekites. Two hundred of his men stayed behind to watch over the equipment and the supplies. When they found the Amalekites, they were feasting and dancing because of all the great spoil they had taken from both the Philistines and the people of Judah. David's army killed them from twilight until the next evening. The only ones who escaped the sword were those who rode off on their camels and fled. *"And David recovered all that the Amalekites had carried away: and David rescued his two wives. And there was nothing lacking to them, neither small nor great, neither sons nor daughters, neither spoil, nor any [thing] that they had taken to them: David recovered all."*

Not only did David recover all he and his men lost, but they also plundered the Amalekites of everything they had. Indeed the thief was found and had to surrender all he had, his entire household, and his very life.

Beloved, this is how God deals with pirates, thieves and invaders. He did it for David and he will do it for anyone who is bold enough to seek him diligently and obtain the great treasure of the kingdom. After all, this is God's property. Your treasure is part of the ancient kingdom dynasty that God is restoring in the earth.

Be bold and courageous, steadfast in your faith. If you are willing and obedient, you shall eat the good treasure of the land.

**He Hath Made Every Thing Beautiful
In His Time:
Also He Hath Set The World In Their Heart,
So That No Man Can Find Out
The Work That God Maketh
From The Beginning To The End.**

**I Know That There Is No Good In Them,
But For A Man To Rejoice,
And To Do Good In His Life.
And Also That Every Man Should
Eat And Drink,
And Enjoy The Good Of All His Labour,
It Is The Gift Of God.**

**I Know That, Whatsoever God Doeth, It Shall
Be For Ever: Nothing Can Be Put To It,
Nor Any Thing Taken From It:
And God Doeth It,
That Men Should Fear Before Him.**

Ecclesiastes 3:11-14 (KJV)

www.ingramcontent.com/pod-product-compliance
Lightning Source LLC
Chambersburg PA
CBHW042310150426
43198CB00001B/28